What Democracy Meant to the Greeks

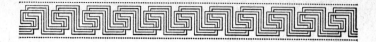

What Democracy Meant
to the Greeks

BY WALTER R. AGARD

CHAPEL HILL · 1942

The University of North Carolina Press

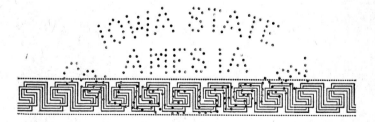

Designed by Stefan Salter
Printed and bound in the United States of America by
American Book-Stratford Press, Inc., New York

TO

WALTER MERRITT AGARD

"... the future, greater than all the past,
Is swiftly, surely preparing for you."

PREFACE

Democracy is a Greek word. The democratic way of life was first formulated and practiced by the Greeks. In the face of Oriental tyranny they proclaimed, and fought successfully to preserve, the superior values of self-governing communities. Among them arose the civil liberties of speech and public assembly. They regarded the state as educational and ethical in its primary purpose rather than military and coercive, and recognized its duty to provide citizens with opportunities for richly varied living. Facing the difficulties of foreign relations, they created an empire controlled by a democracy and confederations of city-states.

In times like these, when democratic institutions have undergone more violent criticism and attack than ever before, it may be useful to re-examine this phase of Greek life: the original evolution of a democratic society, its aims and procedures, the appraisal of its successes and failures by its own critics, the causes of its decline. Since the problems which confronted the Greeks were in many respects similar to ours, it may be that we can still profit from their experience.

To be sure, their leading state, Athens, was different from any of the present time. That was a smaller, less complicated, less experienced world. The immaturities are obvious, especially in economic resources and scientific technology. Conduct lacked the guide of Christian ethics. To a certain extent Athens was not a democracy at all; its economy involved a slave system, although, as we shall see, the notion that it was an aristocratic society favoring the privileged few at the expense of the masses is far from correct. There was only a rudimentary system of representation, with most of the officials chosen by lot; public policy was generally determined by direct vote of the citizens. Other differences between that democracy and ours will appear in the course of this study.

Yet we shall also find interesting and significant similarities in the issues that were faced and the solutions that were reached with more or less success. Certainly many of the psychological and moral factors were like our own, as well as basic political and economic ones. And if in specific ways we shall profit only slightly from their experience, by adopting some of their methods and avoiding their mistakes, there is real value in relating ourselves to the democratic tradition, in appreciating the intelligence and courage of the men who did these things, in feeling comradeship with those first fighters in the age-long struggle to achieve democracy.

It is not the purpose of this book to describe in great detail the political evolution, procedures, or theories of the Greeks. Many excellent books have been written on these subjects. They should be consulted, as well as histories of Greece and the original sources (see the List of Books for Further Reading, on page 267), in order to make the picture complete. This book aims merely to study the human values that were sought and realized by Greek democracy, the chief problems that it faced, the measure of success and failure that resulted, the validity of the criticism of it by its own greatest thinkers.

Many translated passages have been included, in order to let the Greeks speak for themselves. The reader can judge how effectively they spoke. The translations are my own, in some cases abridged and rather freely rendered, with occasional borrowing of apt phrases from other versions.

In the preparation of this book I have received valuable help from my colleagues, Norman O. Brown, Charles F. Edson, A. D. Winspear, Selig Perlman and Carl Boegholt, and from J. P. Harland and Max Kadushin. To them I am deeply grateful. I also wish to acknowledge the courtesy of the *Classical Journal* and the *Dalhousie Review* in permitting me to use some material which I have previously published in those magazines.

My greatest debt remains to be acknowledged. Con-

temporary Greeks, genuinely democratic in spirit, as I
have good reason to know, have shown by their heroic
resistance against aggression that they are still true to the
finest traditions of their past. Nothing could be more
satisfying to a student of ancient Greece than to see how,
regardless of the odds or the immediate consequences,
men who realize what freedom meant to their ancestors
and means to them will fight to preserve it.

WALTER R. AGARD

Madison, Wisconsin
October 19, 1941.

Contents

CHAPTER   PAGE

Preface   vii

Introduction: What Does Democracy Mean?   3

I. PIONEERS

1. The Tribal Age   19
2. Storm and Stress   30
3. The Rise of the Common Man   44

II. ATHENS: DEMOCRACY AND EMPIRE

4. Pericles' Platform   59
5. The Athenian Democracy   69
6. Empire   83
7. Community Art   102
8. The New Education   116
9. Politics and the Drama   127
10. Conceptions of Fate and Freedom   140
11. Intolerance   152
12. The Evolution of a Hero   162

CHAPTER   PAGE

III. THE CRITICISM AND DECLINE OF DEMOCRACY

13. Conservative Reactions   175
14. The Fading Tradition   194
15. Plato's Appraisal   206
16. The Political Science of Aristotle   221
17. Union Then   229
18. Individual Liberty and World-Patriotism   239

CONCLUSION

Looking Forward   255

Chronology   259
Notes   263
List of Books for Further Reading   267
Index   271

Introduction

WHAT DOES DEMOCRACY

MEAN?

At the foundation of the widely differing systems devised by democratic peoples, there is one essential conviction, expressed in the word democracy itself: that power should be in the hands of the people—political power (the concept has often been limited to that), economic power, social power.

This belief has always been challenged and bitterly fought by autocrats and those who consider themselves aristocrats because of superior birth, wealth, culture, or strength of will. According to them, most people are incapable of exercising such power; they lack the necessary intelligence, they are swayed by individual caprice and mass emotion. The self-chosen few have considered the "mob" as people inferior by nature, or even as sub-men, and have either pitied or frankly scorned them. This verdict, the autocrats and aristocrats say, is proved valid by the action of the people when they do exercise control. Democracies have been inefficient, unable or unwilling to make use of the experts who are so necessary, especially in any complicated political and economic system; they have wasted time in endless discussion when speedy decisions were urgently required; they have been stupid or apathetic, so that they have constantly been victimized by so-called public servants. In a word, the mass of men should, in their own interest, be governed by their intelligent and efficient betters.

In the face of this indictment what is the justification for the democratic faith? It is not enough to make merely a negative defense, to say that autocrats and aristocrats have also failed in intelligence, efficiency, and honest public service. Some more positive answer must be given.

Democracy has an answer to give. Admitting its faults and the need for correcting them, it nevertheless claims for itself a fundamental validity that no other kind of society shares; it asserts that creative activity flourishes best when ordinary men have a sense of freedom and responsibility, and extraordinary men work in free association with their fellows. History supports this claim. Our culture is the consequence of such co-operation among men who have recognized their dependence on one another; out of such association developed language, the arts and sciences, social institutions. Whenever there has failed to be a common interchange of ideas through freedom of speech, a common interchange of appreciations through artistic freedom, a common interchange of ideals through freedom of religion, the creative spirit has declined. Autocrats and arbitrary party groups have often controlled men by means of force; they have temporarily operated machines of peace or war with great efficiency; by pressure or patronage they have enlisted the services of able scientists and artists; but they have failed, in the long run, to stimulate human initiative or foster human happiness because they have denied the values which men honor most deeply and most deeply need for living and working.

What are those values? How can democracy give them the best environment in which to flourish? Let us examine specifically the axioms of a creative society and some of the ways in which they can be applied most successfully to human living.

1. Each individual has essential importance and worth as a person. "Life, liberty, and the pursuit of happiness," if not the natural and absolute rights of every one, are at least good for every one; it is good to feel free to live and enjoy oneself in one's own way, free to express oneself without restraint or fear, to worship as one chooses, to have a job that one enjoys doing and to participate in determining the conditions under which one works, to be

free from the fear of arbitrary coercion and oppression. These personal values, which must be regarded as rights unless they are used for anti-social purposes, are superior to those of property or institutions; "the Sabbath was made for man, not man for the Sabbath." It was a profound insight of democracy into human nature that guaranteed for each individual a sphere of liberty to be himself; how profound it was may not be realized by those who take such liberty for granted, but the testimony of refugees from countries in which freedom has been brutally suppressed reveals the tragedy of its loss.

But we must grant that these freedoms may be misused. When personal privilege conflicts with the welfare of the community, when men seek only to satisfy their own desires and become insensitive to the needs of their neighbors, regulation is required. Anarchy is suicidal. Yet it remains true that the primary tenet of democracy is faith in the right of each individual to build for himself the happiest and most complete life of which he is capable.

2. Human nature has qualities of intelligence and good will which can be relied upon. Democracy is optimistic about the ability of men to direct their development by the use of reason. This confidence has obviously been justified in our mastery of nature and in our scientific, technological and artistic skills. In the field of social relationships control has been slower and less certain, because the problems are so much more complicated. But here, too, experience has proved (as we shall

see later) that people can be trusted to work out useful solutions when they have sufficient education and responsibility. Under decent conditions most men may also be counted on to act honestly and in good faith toward others. There is still enough of the wolf in us, however, so that any community must be on its guard against those who may prefer duplicity to fair-dealing.

3. Opportunity is to be provided every person on the basis of his ability, and on that basis alone. Democracy recognizes no validity in the prejudices of class, race, or religion. It regards any standard except that of personal worth not only as unjust to those who are discriminated against, but also as socially harmful in rejecting the contribution which such people could make for the enrichment of all. It may be questioned at this point whether the recognition of individual differences is consistent with the democratic concept of equality, and of course it is not if by equality we mean that all men are born with the same capacity. But no one can reasonably claim that they are. The democratic concept of equality is this: that all men deserve equally to be respected as human beings and given a fair chance to express their ability. But far from disregarding inequalities of talent, democracy glories in them, and is hospitable to variety and differences, realizing how such diversity enriches and vitalizes the common life. It is the authoritarians who advocate the principle that all men (except themselves) have been created equal, on an extremely low level, thereby con-

demning them to regimentation and destroying their creative powers.

4. The welfare of the entire community is the aim of social organization. Collective interests must be protected against any individual or group which jeopardizes them, and every special-interest group must be appraised and treated in terms of its relation to the whole. Since autocrats and aristocrats have sometimes claimed that the welfare of the community is their aim, too, and that they are best fitted to bring it about, we must proceed to the means by which it may be realized.

5. The judgment of all the people, in the long run, is both sounder and safer with respect to the general welfare than that of any one person or group. In government, industry, and social relations alike, absolutism may at times be benevolent but it eventually tends to seek its own interest at the expense of the many, and dangerous social unrest is likely to follow. What Walter Lippmann has said regarding the control of industry applies equally well to other arbitrary rule: "Employers are not wise enough to govern their men with unlimited power, and not generous enough to be trusted with autocracy." [1]

In the short run, it must be granted, the judgment of the people has sometimes been uninformed and capricious. So democracies have usually come to discipline themselves with constitutional checks, which give their judgment time to mature before final action is taken, and to provide for representative government when the community is too large for direct action to seem expedient.

They have also realized the need of using the advice of experts in various fields, but rightly insist that policy-making in an inclusive field can never be delegated to specialists in separate fields; only representatives of the people, directly responsible to them, can wisely be trusted with that function. They have further learned from experience that they cannot afford to ride rough-shod over minorities; the resulting discontent and resentment may threaten the stability of the entire social structure.

6. Sound judgment is most likely to be arrived at by unhampered access to the facts and by general discussion of those facts. Access to correct and adequate information is the first requirement for the forming of any valid judgment. The contribution of many minds to the interpretation of such information is inevitably enriching, as every association of men—scientific, artistic, practical— has demonstrated. Civil liberties are thus to be regarded, not as static safeguards, but as dynamic functions. The unhampered expression of minority opinions is especially important; failure to heed them leads to dogmatism and social sterility.

There are two dangers implicit here: people may make discussion purely a game, a deterrent to action when action needs to be taken promptly, or they may become apathetic and abdicate their responsibility.

In times of crisis, freedom of expression may have to be curtailed if the commonwealth itself is to survive. How extreme must the crisis be to limit a function so individually satisfying and socially useful? A majority decision of the United States Supreme Court some years ago set up the "bad-tendency" test: if any utterance has the tendency to result in criminal action it is illegal. A minority opinion by Justices Holmes and Brandeis dissented on the ground that intention to bring about a criminal act, with a clear and present chance of its success, must be proved. It would seem that neither opinion gave sufficient weight to the social importance of free speech. As Donald Meiklejohn has said,[2] in order to get a common judgment of value we must refuse no contribution which may be offered; we cannot afford to weaken "the resourcefulness that depends on variety and the toughness that issues from resolution of differences"; to suppress even "dangerous" ideas would force underground some points of view that may be worth hearing. In other words, free speech serves a positive purpose in forming sound community judgments, and should be suppressed only in time of extreme crisis. Even then, it may be argued, advocates of any point of view should be tolerated as long as they are willing to present their case candidly for open discussion and to abide by the decisions reached by democratic procedure. And certainly the only agent competent to limit freedom of speech is the government itself.

7. Once these facts are presented and discussed, decisions for action are most wisely made by deliberative vote of the majority. The characteristic method of democracy—the sifting of various opinions, the give and take of argument, the friendly adjustment of differences

—requires patience and tolerance, but it gives the best promise of arriving at acceptable decisions. The alternatives are intrigue and violence, both of which are socially destructive. These tactics of the authoritarians have been sometimes used avowedly to accomplish democratic ends; but democracy recognizes no divorce of ends and means: the end is revealed by the means, and the means which are used determine the end. Democracy is true to itself only when it follows the method of reaching decisions by free discussion and deliberation, and then abides by the will of the majority. It will resort to force only as a temporary necessity against enemies of the democratic process who use violence or intrigue in an effort to destroy it.

8. A community is most productive when all its abilities are utilized. No party, class or faction has a monopoly of talent; we have reason to believe that ordinary people have reserves of skill and competence which have rarely been tapped. It is the first duty of a democracy to devise means for discovering where these talents lie, then educating them and providing for their functioning freely and eagerly.

Rigid schemes of standardization must be avoided. In our economic structure, for instance, it may well be that no single system is adequate to liberate these abilities; that private enterprise, producer and consumer co-operatives, industry partly controlled by labor, and government business may work side by side, each stimulating the others to greater public service and releasing the full productive capacities of their workers.

There is a danger here of jealousy being directed against the abler men, a tendency to check legitimate ambition, a popular distrust of the expert. Men must be educated to maintain a respect for every skill and encourage its working for the common good.

9. Community health, happiness, and progress are achieved by the co-operation of the many, not of the few alone. Men work most effectively and live most zestfully when they engage, not in ruthless competition, but in friendly collaboration, not under the domination of an autocrat, but in the happiness of developing initiative and realizing the value of what they are doing.

Dr. Walter B. Cannon, in his 1940 presidential address before the American Association for the Advancement of Science, drew an interesting physiological analogy. He declared that in a healthy body myriads of differentiated cells are organized into functional organs, all co-operating in a dynamic democracy; that any form of dictatorship by an individual organ, even the brain, will lead to degeneration or death. Tyranny in the body is best illustrated by a tumor, which has its own way for a time but eventually destroys the organism on which it lives. So in a healthy society, all individuals and groups co-operate so as to enable each part to contribute to the welfare of the whole; no individual or group must be allowed to assume domination over others, for if it does the entire social organism will suffer.

It must be granted that democracy is not yet as effective as it must become in solving the complicated social and economic problems that have arisen as a result of its own creative energy, and has been inefficient in directing social and economic machinery. How to do this better is a challenge to the ingenuity of free people. Yet a little immediate efficiency may well be sacrificed for the sake of preserving greater values. A dictator may produce impressive material results, but at the cost of degrading the human spirit. Industrial autocracy may produce more goods, but at a frightful expense in the health and happiness of men, women and children. It is still true, as Thomas Jefferson said, that "the care of human life and happiness is the first and only legitimate object of good government."

We cannot deny, however, that efficiency is important. Its best guarantee is expert leadership. There is every reason to believe, judging from the experience of previous cultures as well as our own, that when they are educated to the need of them democracies can select able leaders and make full use of the skill of trained specialists. And there is beyond question greater opportunity for leadership to reveal itself and be accepted in a free society than under the jealous eye of a dictator or an arbitrary ruling class.

But more than efficiency is required to create a distinguished culture. In the greatest periods of the past this has been the product of people who have developed the sense of sharing in a common enterprise, fusing their diversity of experience into a unity which has transcended party and class. Sometimes a unifying aim has been imposed by individuals or groups from above, who have persuaded or mastered the people by superior will power and clever manipulation. But experience has shown that this unity can also evolve from within, and only when it has done so has it had a substantial basis and liberated a lasting creative energy. For under such circumstances individual freedoms realize their most constructive social value. Freedom of speech means the responsible interchange of ideas and formulation of public policy; freedom of religion means earnest effort to create a better world; economic freedom means working for the improvement, not only of the conditions of labor, but also of means for producing and distributing more and better goods; the freedom from fear leads to social courage. When the members of a community possess this spirit of freely participating in a common cause, the fruits of which they will share, there true democracy functions.

This involves a constantly self-renewing creative effort. No period and no generation can simply inherit the results of previous labor and vision; a society must be dynamic or it will degenerate. Here is a true lesson of history which democracies will disregard at their peril. When people become satisfied, they grow soft; when they take their institutions and officials for granted, those institutions and officials tend to further their own separate interests; when freedom is no longer regarded as a precious thing to be devotedly used, it becomes the plaything of individual caprice until it runs the risk of being destroyed by its enemies. Eternal effort as well as eternal vigilance is the price of liberty.

Universal education is the chief instrument whereby understanding of democratic institutions, loyalty to them, and the will to improve them are woven into the pattern of social life. In order to fulfill its function, education must itself be dynamic in character, not only transmitting the traditional values of our culture but also fearlessly re-examining and restating them in terms of changing conditions. And it must be democratic in its methods as well as its purposes, encouraging free discussion and differences of opinion, and determining its policies by the collaboration of students, teachers, administrators, and the public whom they serve. For unless there is democracy in education, how can there be education for democracy?

We must conclude that unless free people continually re-create their friendly and co-operative unity of spirit, their devotion to a progressive culture, their eagerness for *public* enterprise, their will to protect their institutions against aggression from within as well as from without, they will be (as they have been) the prey of other societies less generous but more determined, less free but fanatically united, less richly varied but more powerful in purpose. Here is a danger to which democracies have many times in the past succumbed, but one which need never frighten them so long as they have the will intelligently and bravely to keep mobilized and on the march all the human resources at their command.

10. Finally, in relations between communities, including international relations, the same principles apply. The soundest and happiest world organization will be based on a recognition of the essential importance and value of each constituent unit; the aim will be the welfare of the entire world; the combined judgment of all states will be superior to that of any one; this judgment is most likely to be reached by unhampered access to the facts and by general deliberation; the world will be most productive when all its capacities are utilized, and this will be achieved by the co-operation of all, united in the sense of sharing a common human enterprise.

On such a foundation can a Community of Nations be built? In this infinitely more complicated field the same difficulties and dangers arise as we have seen in the case of separate communities. But they have already been mastered on a smaller scale with promising results; and democracy has faith that they can eventually be overcome throughout the world, by using the combined human resources of intelligence, good will, and resolute determination.

*   *   *

Such are the values which democracy cherishes. How far they were actually realized in the society which first formulated them we shall now proceed to investigate.

≪ PART ONE ≫

Pioneers

THE TRIBAL AGE

On the plain before the besieged city of Troy, the common man is first represented in the literature of the Western world as asserting his rights.

The episode occurs in the second book of Homer's *Iliad*. A meeting of the general assembly of the army has been called by Agamemnon, commander-in-chief of the expeditionary forces from the Greek tribal states. Realizing that the long years of effort and suffering have sapped the morale of his men, that they need to be aroused to greater ardor if Troy is to be captured, he devises a scheme

to shame them into action; he pretends that he himself
is discouraged, that the venture has been all in vain, and
that they had best sail back home, acknowledging defeat
and dishonor. But the plan was not as sound psychologi-
cally as he believed it would be. The soldiers take him at
his word; they are delighted with the proposal, and rush
enthusiastically to their ships. With great difficulty they
are reassembled. Then a common soldier speaks his mind.

Now all the rest were seated in an orderly fashion in
their places, but Thersites kept babbling on, an endless talker, who had a mind full of subversive ideas
and opposed those in authority with whatever words
he thought would make the soldiers laugh. He was
the ugliest of all the men who came to Troy: bow-
legged, lame in one foot, his two shoulders rounded
and hunched over his chest, and his head rising to a
point with only a little fuzz growing on the top of
it. He was most obnoxious to Achilles and Odysseus,
for he used to revile them constantly; but now it
was noble Agamemnon whom he accused with his
shrill voice. The Achaeans were indignant and disgusted with him, but he kept bawling at the top of
his lungs his criticism of Agamemnon: "Son of
Atreus, what are you finding fault with now, and
what more do you want? Your tents are full of
bronze and many picked women, whom we Achaeans give you first of all whenever we seize a town.
Or don't you think you have gold enough, which
some horse-taming Trojan will bring you as ransom
money for his child, after it was I or some other
soldier who took him prisoner and brought him

here? Or a young girl, for you to keep to yourself
and make love to? (*turning to the soldiers*) I say it
isn't right for our commander to bring misery on us.
Oh you weaklings, cowards, women, not men! Let's
sail home and leave this man here at Troy to enjoy
his precious prizes and find out whether we are of
any use to him or not. Now it's Achilles that he has
dishonored, a much better man than he is; he has
grabbed Achilles' girl and taken her away and kept
her for himself. Achilles doesn't resent it—I'd say he
was slack about that—but if he did (*turning to the
king*), son of Atreus, you would never insult him
again!" [1]

In this speech, bitterly assailing the commander-in-
chief to his face, Thersites is telling at least part of the
truth from the point of view of the soldier in the ranks.
Agamemnon had constantly received special privileges,
and his men had gained little reward except suffering
and death for the service they had rendered. But note
the response to it on the part of both the aristocrats and
the people. Odysseus springs at once to the defense of
his fellow-king, not with arguments but with action:

Noble Odysseus promptly came to his side, glared
at him, and rebuked him sternly: "Thersites, you
babbler, you're a shrill speaker in assembly, but I
tell you to restrain yourself and not be so eager all
by yourself to oppose the kings. I don't believe there
is a viler man than you among all those who came
to Troy with the sons of Atreus. You shouldn't be
talking about kings and criticizing them and watch-

ing for a chance to go back home. We don't know how affairs here are going to turn out. But you persist in reviling Agamemnon, leader of the army, do you, because he has been given so many gifts? I tell you this, and it will happen just as I say, if I find you talking such nonsense again I will forfeit my head and no longer be called father of Telemachos if I don't take hold of you, strip the clothes from your back, whip you out of the assembly, and send you blubbering back to the ships."

Then with his sceptre he hit him on the back and shoulders until Thersites crumpled over with tears rolling down his cheeks. A bloody welt rose up on his back where the gold sceptre had hit him. He sat down, frightened and in pain, realizing the uselessness of what he had done as he wiped away his tears. The people, although they were sorry for him, laughed heartily, and one would say, looking at his neighbor, "Would you believe it! Odysseus has always led the way in council and in the field, but this is by far the best thing he has ever done among us, when he stopped the mouth of this impudent slanderer. Thersites' reckless spirit won't lead him on again to insult our kings." So spoke the people.[2]

Odysseus realized that such sentiments as Thersites' must be checked at once, but he also saw that the man had insufficient support from his fellows to make him actually dangerous. To humiliate him and make him ridiculous was obviously the best strategy. And the people, ashamed of their self-appointed spokesman and aware of the superior power of their leaders, at once dissociated themselves from him. One is reminded of the words of Walt Whitman: "As I stand aloof and look there is to me something profoundly affecting in large masses of men following the lead of those who do not believe in men." This may not, however, be quite fair to the people. It must be remembered that the *Iliad* was recited at the courts of princes, and the poet may have added to a traditional story an ending satisfactory to his audience.

What was the social structure in which such an episode could take place?

There is some difficulty in visualizing this society, because the poem in its final form was composed considerably later than the period which it portrays. To disentangle the social customs belonging to the age of tribal migrations, which the *Iliad* chiefly records, from those representing the poet's own time is far from easy. Thus it is possible that the fact of a commoner speaking like Thersites in assembly goes back to a primitive kind of democracy, and the reaction to his speech is typical of the poet's contemporary aristocratic point of view. But this problem need not greatly concern us; for our purposes we may study the way of life pictured in both the *Iliad* and the *Odyssey* as broadly representative of the twilight of Greek tribal society.

Those roving warriors, who had swept down from the northwest into Greece and on to Asia Minor in quest of plunder, had the simple economy, largely agricultural and pastoral, of a tribal order. The *Iliad*, as a story centered about military exploits, gives few details about ordinary daily life, but there is enough information (especially in the description of the Shield of Achilles [3]) to build up the picture fairly well. We read of shepherds with flocks of sheep and men tending oxen, of farmers ploughing, reaping, and cultivating vines. There is some reason to believe that land was owned by the tribe in common, and one got a share as long as one worked to earn it, or it may be that the kings apportioned it on that basis. Judged from the description of the shield itself, decorated with silver, tin and gold, craftsmanship had developed to a high degree of competence; and the excavations of these early sites have revealed how highly developed and exquisite this work really was. There are a few references to slaves, who were captives of war.

The *Odyssey* pictures a rather more complicated economic system. Alcinoüs and Odysseus both have large personal estates, with war captives, men and women, serving them as slaves. Relations between master and slave appear to have been very friendly, the owner and his family often working side by side with the slaves; witness the princess Nausicaä helping her servant girls do the family washing, and Odysseus sowing and reaping along with his men. There is private property; the larger estates are owned by the king and the heads of the great families, his noble vassals, and small ones are owned by independent farmers; there is also a large class of vagrant day laborers who own virtually no property. The craftsman class is increasing; it includes artisans of many kinds. The fact that queens weave and kings are carpenters indicates the respectability of the craftsman's job. But the most significant economic development is the beginning of exchange of goods between foreign traders and the Greek princes, who, by bartering the products of the farms and craftsmen's shops of their native towns with an alien mercantile class, led the way to the development of business as a profession in Greece. In such economic groups we find the essential pattern of later Greek communities, although as yet there is little evidence of the competing interests that were to breed bitter social antagonism a century later.

In political organization, also, the tribal age has elements which were modified but not wholly discarded in the classical period. Each tribal king, to be sure, has supreme command, resting largely in the *Iliad* on his military prowess, in the *Odyssey* on his social and political sagacity; his position is further protected by his function as guardian of traditional customs and religious rites. But the king must consult his council of nobles before he determines any policy of importance, and then must bring the decision to a general assembly of all the citizens to get their opinion. It may be argued that the general assembly, probably having no formal vote, lacked any actual power; but at least it offered the educational value of public discussion, and undoubtedly in turbulent times the king and nobles worked hard to justify their policy before the people, knowing that popular disapproval would jeopardize or ruin the chances of its success.

Here is the germ of the democratic principle: government with the uncoerced consent of the governed. Furthermore, there was apparently complete freedom of speech in the assembly for ordinary men, no matter how critical or even abusive they might be toward their king and the nobles. It was at an assembly of this sort that Thersites went perhaps a step too far and suffered for it; but the amazing thing is that he was allowed to speak at all as he did. There could be no better evidence of an essential democracy in early Greek life.

The religious concepts of the people were a reflection of their social organization. Toward their gods, regarded as a noble group like their own and headed by Zeus the king, they looked with reverence due the immortals, but also with the intimacy inspired by men and women essentially like themselves. They believed that the gods were often at variance with one another, some fighting with them and others with their enemies, and engaging in domestic disputes in heaven like theirs on earth. But even above the gods there was the power of Destiny, from the decrees of which no man, however brave in battle or distinguished for wisdom, regardless of his rank or station, could escape. Living under the constant threat of Destiny's ultimate blow, men could only hope and work to win as much glory as possible before death came.

In the late tribal society the social virtues were in many respects of a high type. Physical courage was of course the outstanding excellence while the people were at war, so Achilles, the foremost fighter, was properly the hero of the *Iliad*, even though to us the statesmanlike

Hector may seem more admirable. But the courage of
the heroes was tempered with kindness; there was a code
of gentlemanly conduct in accordance with which men
tried to live. In battle poison arrows were taboo, the bodies of the slain and the conquered were usually treated
with consideration, captives could be saved from slavery
by ransom, and there were truces for the burial of the
dead. Foes had respect for their opponents; we read of
men fighting bitterly until the day's end, then giving
gifts to each other and parting, for a time, "reconciled in
friendship." They also showed a touching deference to
old people, and received suppliants, ambassadors and
other guests with cordial hospitality.

By the time of the *Odyssey* other virtues were more
necessary: the resourcefulness of mind and stamina of
spirit which Odysseus showed in mastering complex new
situations and dealing with many sorts of alien people.
The admiration shown the Phaeacians for their accom-
plishments in commerce, sports and the amenities of
peace also indicates a new set of social values. In both
epics the quality which restrained the powerful from brutality and the shrewd from greed was *aidos*—profound
self-respect and respect for others is perhaps as adequate
a translation as can be given. When Hector used the
word in his poignant farewell to Andromache, his wife,
trying to persuade her that he must go out and fight even
at the cos of death, it meant a decent regard for public
opinion, a sense of social obligation. Along with this was
the conviction that it is the duty of the privileged to be

generous as well as brave, courteous and hospitable as well as canny, and, above all, to be loyal to the interests of their group. In this respect Achilles was far from perfect. His essentially tragic experience developed as a result of his selfish pride. He was justified in deeply resenting the insult to his honor and in punishing Agamemnon for it, but when he refused to accept Agamemnon's apology and rich gifts of propitiation, and when the defeat of his comrades in arms failed to move him, then he aroused the righteous indignation of his fellows. Even more startling is the frank revelation of the petty as well as the more heinous vices of the suitors for Penelope's hand. Princes and nobles though these men were, they were never praised, and were eventually punished with death for their greed, their cruelty, their lack of *aidos*.

But such criticism must not be regarded as any expression of popular resentment. The poems, composed in an aristocratic age for recital at the courts, exemplified to their audience the code of noble men and deplored actions which violated that code. What the ordinary people did or were was as yet hardly worthy of mention; all that was asked of them was obedience and loyalty. These standards of noble conduct we shall find still applied in later times, but no longer confined to the upper class. By the fifth century B.C., the children of the people were studying the *Iliad* and the *Odyssey*, learning to emulate the courage of Achilles and the nimble wit, curiosity, and endurance of Odysseus, and many of those upper-class ideals had been woven into the social pattern of the democracy.

For an adequate understanding of the relation of tribal society to the later Athenian culture, one final observation must be made before we leave this period. Both the racial stock and the culture patterns of later Greece were founded on a mingling of the northern invaders and the Mediterranean people who inhabited the territory before they came. Only in recent years have we come to realize, owing to archaeological discoveries, how greatly Greek civilization was indebted to the highly developed commercial and artistic society already existing in that area, especially on the island of Crete, during the early infiltration of the northern tribes. The southern tradition, weakened for a time, was later revived chiefly in Ionia; the northern persisted in the Dorian settlements of central and Italiot Greece; but we shall find the finest expression of the Greek genius in the synthesis of the two which was ultimately made in Athens.

STORM AND STRESS

From the end of the tribal age to the first experimental democracy in the sixth century B.C., there was a period of difficult adjustment to new conditions of living. Each of the hundreds of towns which had sprung up in the valleys and on the coast of Greece and Asia Minor and on the little islands of the Aegean Sea had its own particular problems; and as they developed into city-states the topography of the country continued to dictate to them a large measure of political self-sufficiency. But one condition they shared: the poverty of the land, which was not fertile enough to support a growing population. And since much of the land was in the hands of the traditional noble families, there was constant suffering and discontent on the part of the small independent farmers.

We are fortunate in having the observations of one of these farmers in the writings of Hesiod, a Boeotian who lived toward the end of the eighth century B.C. Facing a world in which the wealth of the few had made them arrogant and cruel, and the poverty of the many had reduced them to distrust of one another, petty dishonesty and despair, he condemned it bitterly. Long ago, he surmised, there had been a happy golden age, but now men live in an age of iron. In their degradation they never cease from toil; friendly relations no longer exist between people ("Even with your brother, smile, but get a witness"); the young neglect and scorn their elders; robbery and perjury are rife; the observance of fair-dealing and *aidos* has disappeared. Insolent evil-doers become rich and honored. Might is regarded as right, and there is no help for honest men. He compared those who exercise power to a hawk which has seized a nightingale and bears it aloft in its talons; to the nightingale's entreaties it says:

> You wretch, why do you complain? One far stronger than you has hold of you, and you must go wherever I take you. He is a fool who wills to oppose those who are more powerful; he never wins, and in addition to defeat he suffers humiliating misery.[1]

What can the plain people, weak as they are, do when

they face oppressors who have such superior resources? Hesiod offers two solutions. By painstaking work they can make the best of a cruel world; they can learn how to wrest the last bit of produce from their mean little farms; by keen competition in efficient workmanship, by being thrifty, avoiding debt, planning for the future, helping their neighbors and keeping their promises, they can get on tolerably well with their comrades in misfortune. And by sacrificing to the gods it may be that they will get some help from heaven. For Hesiod cherishes the hope that human injustice is not disregarded by the gods; "the immortals are close to men and they observe those who with crooked judgments grind their fellow men down." So he warns the "bribe-devouring judges" to be fair, the rapacious nobles to mend their ways, lest the gods visit vengeance on them. Force, he concludes, is the rule of animals, but to men Zeus has given the principle of justice, which is a far better way of life even though temporarily it seems to bring little success to those who practice it. Hesiod seems more confident of the doom of the unrighteous than of any bliss for the godly.

Here, as in Homer, we see outspoken criticism of the noble families, but now it is from a genuine representative of the underprivileged, who protests, not on personal grounds, but against a social order; and a divine principle of justice is declared superior to the human rule of superior might. But the language of protest was not translated into any program of effective action. In fact, the peasants were advised to make the best of their present lot, in the tenuous hope that ultimately the gods would redress the balance.

That this was the prevailing attitude of the common people is further indicated by the rapid spread of a new popular religion imported from the east toward the end of the eighth century B.C. The religion of the heroic age had been the Olympian cults described in the Homeric poems; people worshiped with sacrifices and prayer a heavenly tribal order similar to earthly ones, with Zeus the king surrounded by his noble vassal gods and goddesses. This faith offered no immortality that men would desire, no life after death except the shadowy existence of souls flitting about in the gloom of Hades, deprived of the bodies which had made mortal life so glorious; in the *Odyssey* the soul of Achilles declares that it would rather live in the world of men as a day laborer serving a man without property (no mortal existence could seem meaner to Achilles than that), than be king among the shades below. This continued to be the official religion of the city-states; but now the new religion of Dionysus appeared, with a greater appeal to the masses of the people. The god Dionysus was not an aristocrat; he, too, had been scorned and rejected and had suffered anguish; he had no reproach for the unprivileged, but gave them his wine which freed them from pain and fear. And he offered them hope. He was a vegetation god, whom they could worship in the expectation that their crops would give a greater yield. And, above all, he promised a blessed immortality which the humblest of his followers would enjoy, in which they would find release from their earthly frustration and misery, and win a life that was divinely happy like that of their victorious god. Small wonder that this religion found an enthusiastic following among the common people!

Closely related to the Dionysiac cults were other mystery religions which developed rapidly at this time; those of Demeter and Persephone at Eleusis and the Orphic rites won disciples in many parts of the Greek world. The Eleusinian mysteries included a picturesque ritual which gave worshipers who participated in it the assurance of immortal bliss. Followers of Orpheus placed greater emphasis on dogma and conduct. According to their faith all men possess an earthly part, the body, and a divine one, the soul; the chief object of life is to suppress one's lower nature and, by observing an ascetic regimen, cleanse the soul of earthly stain. As time went on, the control of the cult by an increasingly powerful group of priests and their insistence on an esoteric creed and exacting dietetic restrictions resulted in a loss of interest on the part of the common people; by nature neither fanatics nor ascetics, and too independent and ambitious to surrender to domination by priests, they preferred the more tolerant mystery religions. Consequently Orphism became centered in exclusive religious brotherhoods.

Moral and religious anodynes, however, could not check the ferment of social change. The conflict between aristocrats and the masses grew more critical throughout the Greek world. Economic inequality based on the ownership of land steadily increased, the few reducing the many to a state of virtual serfdom. In the seventh century B.C., the invention of coined money accelerated the cleavage. Many of the noble families, clever in utilizing this new instrument of acquisition, increased their holdings. But the introduction of coined money was most important in building up a new class of privileged people: the merchants, traders, and manufacturers. The development of new markets required export goods, which were supplied by increasing the output of oil and wine and objects of craftsmanship; this in turn led to the expansion of slave labor at home and the establishment of colonies abroad, the settlement of which relieved temporarily the overpopulation of the mother cities.

As a result of this economic process, the mercantile class rose rapidly in importance, challenging the prestige of the old aristocratic landholding families; but the peasant farmers, lacking capital for the development of their farms or even for maintenance during bad years, forced to borrow at high rates of interest and eventually mortgage their farms and even offer their own persons as security, were being driven to a state of slavery. Day laborers were also being exploited by employers who had an increasing supply of slaves at their command. In consequence the gulf between rich and poor, between the privileged and the exploited, grew steadily larger; discontent increased among the lower classes, until it flared into hatred. Meanwhile the merchants, jealous of the political power of the large landowners, were ready to join a coalition against them. The situation was ripe for revolution; all that was lacking was leadership.

This leadership was supplied by the emergence of so-called tyrants in many parts of the Greek world during the seventh and sixth centuries B.C. They were men of superior ability, usually members of aristocratic families, who, because of feuds with other nobles, the desire to further their business interests, personal ambition, or a genuine concern for the welfare of the city and the people, organized their personal armies and overthrew the established oligarchical governments. Their own practice of government, ostensibly and for the most part actually in the interest of the oppressed, was autocratic to varying degrees. In the early Greek sense of the word, tyranny meant simply rule acquired and held by unconstitutional means, and the exercise of such power was oppressive chiefly in that it restricted the control formerly held by the nobility. Often the tyrant was aided to power by a coalition of the masses and the new business interests, both of which desired the overthrow of the traditional aristocracy, and his rule was usually conciliatory in character, since its continuance depended on avoiding too bitter resentment on the part of any class. But to avoid resentment on the part of the old nobility, as they saw their ancestral privileges wrested from their hands, was next to impossible; the ambition of the mercantile class was difficult to keep in check; and the plain people were still not satisfied with their economic status. So the lot of the tyrants was, at best, not a very happy one. That they lived in constant fear of ambitious rivals is indicated by the advice attributed to Periander of Corinth, to cut down all stalks of grain that tower above the rest. They made a great contribution, however, by limiting the power of the old oligarchy; thus they were the forerunners of popular government.

In the lyric poems of the period we find a revealing record of the turbulent events and men's reaction to them. The fact that poets were now voicing their own judgment on the contemporary world rather than singing of the heroic past is itself an indication of the new spirit of the times; and in their emphasis on the right of the individual to find happiness in his own way they contributed a liberalizing influence: Archilochus, the roving soldier of fortune, praising the adventurous life; Mimnermus proclaiming the validity of the pursuit of pleasure; Sappho creating uninhibited expression for her inner experience. Although most of them were from aristocratic families and might have been expected to oppose the rising power of the mercantile class and the people, only a few expressed themselves on politics, but those who did so were violently partisan. The career of Alcaeus of Mitylene is characteristic of the politically-minded poets. When he was a young boy his brothers led in the overthrow of a tyrant, and Alcaeus himself fought unsuccessfully against the later tyrant, Myrsilus, in the civil war that raged at the end of the seventh century. In exile he wrote a poem which compared his country to a ship lashed by furious winds; in such a storm what can a noble person do, he asks, except drink to drown his sorrows and resolve to be loyal to the good old virtues which shall yet save the ship of state? After the death of Myrsilus, Alcaeus came to terms for a time with the succeeding tyrant, Pittacus. Pittacus was a man of the people, of whom the millers sang as they worked:

> Grind, mill, grind,
> For Pittacus, too, grinds his grain,
> The ruler of great Mitylene.

He wisely tried to reconcile the differences between the conflicting elements in his city. But Alcaeus was temperamentally unable to endure such a compromise with his aristocratic ideals, and soon was insulting the tyrant as "base-born," describing his physical ugliness and his unsavory habits, and foretelling the ruin of the country under his leadership. He was again banished, but toward the end of Pittacus' ten years of rule received amnesty along with his fellow exiles.

Another opponent of democratic development, more vehement in his antagonism, was Theognis, a noble who suffered from the death of his friends and the loss of his property in the civil wars of Megara. Who can endure, he wrote, seeing base men in power, the shameless rabble ruling, the crew of the ship of state in mutiny seizing command and plundering the cargo? These men who used to troop to town dressed in skins and hides, docile as cattle and unaware even that laws exist, now have control over us and have reduced us to poverty and impotence. Believing that the popular revolt was due to the inertia, lack of courage, and compromising attitude of the aristocrats, he exhorted them to revive their ancient virtues of loyalty to their class, honor, and fighting spirit, and to add to these a new diplomacy and ruthlessness. Beguile your enemy with fine words, he said, but when you get him in your power don't spare him; trample on the empty-headed mob, whip and yoke them; that is the treatment they understand and really like; if necessary, assassinate their leaders. "Oh, let me drink the dark blood of those enemies who robbed me of my property!" was his savage conclusion.

Such, in fact, were the tactics which the gentlemen of Megara and the other cities during those days of revolution used in an effort to retain their power, and throughout a long period of civil war they at times succeeded. But against the rising tide of democracy their methods had little chance of ultimate success.

Other poets, less partisan and inflexible, found it agreeable to live under the patronage of the tyrants, and abandoned political verse for the less dangerous themes of love and wine. Foremost among them were Ibycus, who accepted the hospitality of Polycrates, tyrant of Samos, and Anacreon, who drifted from one tyrant's court to another, writing popular songs. It was now the aristocrats rather than the ordinary people who were finding refuge from their frustration, in the anodyne of enjoying the good things of life which they could still salvage from the wreckage of their former largess.

A further reflection of the prevailing economic and political unrest is seen in the speculation of the first philosophers. Some of them, in general sympathy with the trend of the times, challenged traditional beliefs and began to interpret the universe in terms of change and process. Others, doubtless feeling a sense of profound insecurity as they saw their familiar world in danger of alteration, either tried to justify the *status quo* by associating it with universal principles, or, when changes came, sought consolation in their turn as the plain people and the poets had done. The people had found theirs in the mystery religions, the poets in singing of love and wine and adventure; but these philosophers, intellectually more exacting, satisfied their need by conceiving the universe as essentially invariable, set in a pattern of permanence, and by characterizing as illusory what our senses tell us is change.

In philosophy, as in lyric poetry, the Ionian cities took the lead, owing to the faster tempo of development in that part of the Greek world. In Ionia were sea-ports inviting exploration and commerce and located within easy reach of challenging markets; there farming soon became less rewarding than trade. As a result of the prevailing spirit of adventure, which was rapidly weaving new social and economic patterns, inquisitive men became fascinated by the problem of the relation of permanence to process and tried to solve it on intellectual grounds. What is the material of which the world is made? they asked. How can we account for the fact that it assumes so many constantly changing forms? Are there principles in accordance with which this process works? What relation have they to traditional interpretations?

To examine their answers in detail would be outside the range of this study, but some of their attitudes and conclusions have social implications which cannot be ignored, especially their attack on conventional religion, their faith in human reason, and their belief in an evolutionary process.

Anaximander surmised that man had developed from a primitive aquatic form. Xenophanes, dismissing anthropomorphic conceptions of the gods as ridiculous, stated his belief that "by investigation we discover all things," thus dealing a severe blow to the Orphic claims of divine revelation. He also criticized the morals of the gods as described by Homer and Hesiod. From the observation of fossils in rocks he deduced that the earth had gone through a process of change before reaching its present condition.

Perhaps the most profound of the Ionian philosophers was Heraclitus, who declared that the essential quality of life is change. "Everything is in a state of flux," caused by a never-ending strife between opposites; the only permanence lies in a principle of balance which keeps any one factor from securing too great or long-continued dominance. This obviously has social relevance as a warning against excessive power being allowed to get in the hands of any one class. The fragments of his philosophy which scornfully deny the intelligence of the masses (they are evil, they lack wisdom, they say "Let there be no best man among us") suggest that he was apprehensive lest the scales should tip very far in that direction.

Regardless of the political views of these early scientists, such speculation led to the liberation of men's minds and provided a congenial environment for the intellectual developments which followed. By the fifth century Democritus was expounding the atomic theory, Empedocles was distinguishing four elements, Anaxagoras was positing a "mind" in the universe that was merely a kinetic sort of matter, and Hippocrates, a genuinely scientific doctor, having denied that there are any diseases sent by the gods, was methodically studying the process of change in the condition of his patients. It is perhaps significant that many of these men were political liberals. Democritus believed in the principle of equality, Empedocles helped overthrow the oligarchy in Agrigentum, and Anaxagoras was a close friend of Pericles.

But the Ionian interpretations of an evolving world were by no means universally accepted. In the cities of Southern Italy, where Dorian institutions were firmly implanted, where a dominant nobility was entrenched in power and rich lands favored a conservative agricultural economy, and where temperaments were less volatile, there was a vigorous defense by intellectuals of the thesis that the world is essentially unchanging. The doctrines of the Pythagoreans and Eleatics may be understood, partly at least, in the light of social patterns which were congenial to the philosophers; these thinkers were not unaffected in their theorizing about eternal values by the actual political structure of which they were a part.

The Pythagoreans interpreted the world in terms of order and symmetry, based on fixed mathematical ratios, and found a similar satisfactory order and symmetry in existing aristocratic schemes of government. Adopting the Orphic faith, they used it likewise to justify their social theory. As the body must be held in subjection by the soul, so in every society there must be wise and benevolent masters over obedient and grateful inferiors—and of course they had no doubt as to who were qualified to be the masters. Their religious brotherhoods became a powerful political influence in Italiot Greece, a training school for aristocratic leadership.

The Eleatics tried to demonstrate that change is an illusion. There are two ways of life, Parmenides said, one of opinion, the other of truth. Opinion regards the apparently variable world as real, but truth assures us that Being is eternal and unchanging. Justice "holds everything fast." It is significant that he was not merely an abstract philosopher; he also wrote the code of law for his own city in order to stabilize its life. And Zeno, who defended the same thesis by a clever series of paradoxes, is recorded as having opposed a popular leader who was probably no match for him in argument, but did have a conviction that changes were advisable, whether or not a theory of change could be proved by an intellectual demonstration.

THE RISE OF THE

COMMON MAN

There were interesting developments toward democracy in many parts of the Greek world, but since the Athenian experiment was the most far-reaching in its consequences we shall confine ourselves chiefly to its evolution from this point on.

Athens went through the same economic changes which we have already surveyed, but without the extreme violence which elsewhere often accompanied the rise of the mercantile and laboring classes and their undermining the power of the landowning aristocrats.

Among several reasons for the relatively peaceful revolution in Athens, one is doubtless the fact that the late tribal invasions of the Dorians, with their stern subjection of the local inhabitants whom they conquered, never penetrated into Athens. An important factor was the rapid expansion of trade, which resulted in opportunities for the surplus farm population to be absorbed in city craftsmen's shops. Another was the emergence of liberal leaders during periods of crisis.

In the early days the chief communities in the territory of Attica became fused into a unified state with Athens as its capital city. This may have occurred under the leadership of King Theseus, who, according to tradition, was a benevolent and democratically minded ruler. When, at the beginning of the sixth century B.C., the plight of the peasants became acute and it was realized that revolution threatened, another wise leader met the situation with far-sighted common sense. This was Solon, himself of a wealthy family, who by general consent was given temporary dictatorial powers as an arbitrator to relieve the distress of the dispossessed. He has properly been called the father of democracy. By prompt and decisive action he restored self-respect to the desperate farmers and laid the foundations for the future democratic constitution.

First he cancelled all debts which involved the security of a man's person, and made it illegal for such security to be asked or given thereafter. He proceeded to fix limits on the amount of land that any one person could own, and restricted the display of wealth. From a fragment of his writings we gather that he considered an excess of money to be the root of at least many evils. These economic reforms were of a moderate sort, satisfying neither the rich who wanted debts paid in full nor the poor who demanded a complete redistribution of land, but they were adequate to remedy the acute disbalance of the Athenian economic structure. His political reforms were also moderate, but they carried far-reaching implications. Office was still open only to the upper economic orders, but the poorest class was now given a voice in the election of officials and participation in courts which reviewed and judged the acts of the magistrates.

But it was more than the specific reforms of Solon that brought harmony to a distraught community. The character of the man was also responsible for restoring confidence. It will be useful to examine somewhat in detail the qualities that made him an effective popular leader.

First must be accounted the intellectual curiosity and fair-mindedness which refused to be fettered by class prejudice or custom. In his youth he engaged in trade, according to Plutarch, more to get experience and knowledge of the world than to make money, and even in his old age he himself wrote, "I grow old always learning many new things." Plato in the *Timaeus* records an incident which confirms the fact that Solon never outgrew an engaging curiosity and enthusiasm; in the course of his travels in Egypt a venerable priest said to him, perhaps enviously, "Oh, Solon, Solon, you Greeks are always children. There isn't an old man among you, you are all young in spirit." [1] And in his declining years he came to realize even the good that the tyrant Pisistratus was doing for the common people of Athens.

Next was a genius for reconciling differences, certainly one of the chief requirements for democratic leadership. He allied himself with neither the rich nor the poor, but kept the respect of the rich because of his wealth and won the respect of the poor because of his obvious honesty and desire to help them. When urged to assume tyrannical power he refused, on the ground that he had no faith in violence. Tyranny is doubtless a lovely situation to be in, he said ironically, but it has no exit. He preferred instead to be able to say this: "I have given the common people sufficient power to assure them of dignity, and I have protected those of great wealth and influence. I took a firm stand, holding my stout shield over both classes, so that neither should win any unfair advantage." Here for the first time the theory was stated that government is an impartial arbiter, reconciling conflicting interests. "Equality," he declared, meaning equality before the law, "breeds no revolution." When his hopes were ridiculed by a visitor, who denied that injustice and greed could be checked by laws, since like spiders' webs they restrained the weak but were easily broken by the strong, Solon replied that his aim was to demonstrate that the practice of justice was actually more profitable than its violation. He also had a keen sense of practical politics. When asked if he had enacted the best laws, he said, "The best that could have been acceptable to the people." The Greek virtue of moderation was never better realized than by Solon.

He won leadership because he respected the common virtues: family devotion and a sense of private and public decency. Property rights he genuinely held as inferior to human rights; in fact the love of wealth he considered essentially vulgar. This is illustrated by Herodotus' charming account of his visit to Croesus, the fabulously wealthy king of Lydia.[2] Croesus, after entertaining Solon by displaying his treasures, asked him whom he considered the happiest man he had ever met, expecting to be properly congratulated; but Solon named instead a simple Athenian who had led a normal life with his family and met death bravely fighting for his country; next to him he named two Argive lads who died after showing surpassing devotion to their mother. In his writings we find this comment: "Often unjust men are rich and just men poor, but we will not exchange our virtue for their money, since excellence is a lasting thing, but wealth changes owners constantly."

What was "our virtue"? Personal honesty and a sense of social duty. That city is best, he declared, in which men who are not wronged exert themselves to punish a wrongdoer. He enacted a law providing that every one in time of public controversy must take sides on pain of being disfranchised, on the principle that no man must be so concerned about his private affairs that he is indif-

ferent to the public welfare; another law aimed to promote friendlier relations by making slander a crime.

Finally, he had great courage: courage not to make too
great concessions to the powerful in fear of what they
might do to him, or to accede to the excessive demands
of those who chose him as their champion. "I combine
justice and force," he declared, realizing that all the good
will in the world is ineffective without prompt and decisive action. And he won his way, not by flattery, but by
candor; he made the people face their faults. It was fortunate indeed that in such a time of emergency Athens
found such a leader.

In spite of Solon's efforts, however, the cure was not a
permanent one. It had removed the most flagrant economic injustice, but it failed to provide an adequate program of opportunity for the people; and in the wake of
the moderate political reforms there was renewed party
strife. Following the customary Greek pattern, a tyrant
came into power during the last half of the sixth century
B.C. Organizing his own army, consisting chiefly of the
poorest peasants with the co-operation of some members
of the mercantile class, Pisistratus established order by
setting up a system which, while retaining in general the
framework of previous procedures, made the aristocrats
ineffective by placing them under his control. He was, it
may be said, the first Athenian practical politician in the
modern sense of the word. Realizing that his continuance in power depended on popular approval, he offered
the people what the nobility had never had either the

wish or the sense to provide; he encouraged small industries and commerce; he stimulated trade by importing expert craftsmen; he instituted a program of public works to improve living conditions and beautify the city; he created more interesting and varied festivals for their enjoyment, and arranged for the recital of the *Iliad* and the *Odyssey* at the greatest of the religious festivals, the Panathenaea, to aid in making Athens a cultural capital. As a result of this genuine public service he remained in power, except for two periods of exile, until his death. The people knew that he had made life richer and more productive for them, and they appreciated it.

Why, then, did the tyranny collapse so soon after his death? Partly because his sons lacked his political and social genius; they failed to realize that their power was contingent on their using it in ways acceptable to the people, and turned it instead to their own purposes. Partly because they were no longer needed; the power of the aristocrats had been seriously weakened. Most of all, perhaps, because the majority of business and working people had been educated to a sense of their own importance and were now ready to control the institutions of the city.

This they did under the leadership of Cleisthenes in the final years of the sixth century. Like so many leaders of democratic movements in Athens, he came from a noble family, but he understood the trend of the times and chose to direct rather than oppose it. The first need was to destroy the factionalism based on old group loyalties. Cleisthenes worked out a scheme of geographical distribution which cut across the former divisions, and formed new units each one of which included representatives from all of the former class groups of small and large landholders, business men and craftsmen, and workers on the coast. Thus by a shrewd administrative device people of different classes and conditions were forced to act in common. One can imagine that men in those days criticized the scheme on the ground that human nature can never be changed, but Cleisthenes apparently did change it. The new constitution which was adopted provided for participation of more citizens of Athens in its government on a basis of equality. The public assembly became the law-making body; the chief executive functions were entrusted to a representative people's council of five hundred members, chosen annually by lot, fifty from each of the new units; judicial functions were controlled by people's juries, selected from an annual panel of six thousand citizens chosen by lot from the same units. Minor executive officials were also chosen by lot from the roster of citizens; only the Board of Generals was elected. More important than the actual machinery of government was the principle which was responsible for it: that all Athenians hereafter should share in the control of their way of living. Democracy had at last come into its own.

It was chiefly due to this responsible and confident citizenry that the invasion of Greece by the Persian armies and navy was repelled at Marathon and Salamis.

The reason why the seeming miracle was accomplished is indicated by Herodotus, the historian of the Persian wars. The King of Persia, he writes, was governed by outrageous pride (*hybris*), employing subject peoples to accomplish his will. Such absolute rulers, being answerable only to themselves, oppress their people and make them weak in spirit. But the Greeks were strong because among them liberty and equality were considered the most important things in the world. He pictures the Athenians replying to agents of the Persian King: "We know as well as you do that the power of your king is far greater than our own. Nevertheless, because we love liberty, we shall fight as best we can." [3] It was not by chance that the Athenians had the courage to make a reply like that. Herodotus explains: "So the Athenians increased in strength. It is obvious, not from their example only, but from many others, that freedom is a good thing; for even the Athenians, as long as they were under a tyrant's yoke, were not one bit braver than any of their neighbors, but as soon as they shook off their yoke they became by far the first. While living under oppression they let themselves be beaten, because they were working for a master; but when they won their freedom each man wanted to do the best he could, because he knew that he would enjoy the fruits of his effort." [4] Herodotus makes it clear that they had more than the will to win. They had also prepared intelligently under the leadership of the democrat, Themistocles, by building up their naval strength to the full extent of their resources.

Although Herodotus showed in many instances his aversion to absolute government and was obviously less than fair to Pisistratus, it is impossible to discover just where his own sympathies lay. In one passage he describes a debate in which representatives of monarchy, oligarchy and democracy present the claims for those systems of government. The democrat argues that government should be in the hands of all the people, because the rule of one man is neither just nor agreeable; answerable to nobody, he becomes arrogant, oppressive, jealous of the best citizens, the prey of flatterers and sycophants, lawless. In a democracy, however, the people enjoy and profit from sharing responsibility. The oligarch admits that monarchy is bad, but declares that it is equally disastrous to entrust government to the people, who are ignorant and wayward and who themselves become oppressive. It is best for the ablest citizens to rule (they of course include us, he says), for their wise counsel will serve the best interests of all. Monarchy is then urged on the ground that small ruling groups develop strife among themselves in their ambition for power, and in a democracy pressure groups are formed which stop at nothing in trying to get what they want for themselves; the one wisest man should have supreme power. Herodotus did not take sides, and in view of his wide experience in sympathetically recording the local customs of many places he doubtless held that no single policy of government would suit all people; but it is likely that he favored a moderate democratic constitution, in which the popular will was held in firm check and in which there was a deep respect for established customs, a government of laws rather than of men.

The leading poets who celebrated the victory over Persia were Simonides and Aeschylus. Aeschylus' play, the *Persians*, was entirely devoted to this theme, picturing the dismay at the Persian court when news of the defeat of Xerxes' armada at Salamis was announced. It includes the stirring battle-song of the Greek sailors as their fleet took the offensive in the early dawn:

> On, sons of Greece, free your fatherland, free your children, your wives, the shrines of your ancestral gods, the tombs of your forefathers. Now is the supreme struggle for everything we cherish.[5]

The moral lesson which Aeschylus drew from the invasion which failed was summed up in this judgment on Xerxes: "Pride, after it blossoms, produces fruit of doom and a harvest of tears."

Simonides, an Ionian poet who spent a good part of his life in Athens, was the poet laureate, so to speak, of the period of the Persian wars; the best of his tributes praise the men who fought at Marathon, Thermopylae, Salamis and Plataea. In terse couplets he declared that the Spartans at Thermopylae, like good soldiers, died while obeying orders; of the Athenians who fell at Marathon and Salamis he wrote:

> If the man who does what is best is rightfully honored, it is the people of Athens alone who deserve

credit for having carried this thing through . . . They took the lead in fighting for Greece, they scattered the might of Persia and its wealth . . . The sons of Athens saved their land from bitter slavery.

For the heroes of Plataea he composed this tribute:

If to die nobly is the greatest good one can do one's country, to us of all men Fortune gave this boon; for, eager to crown Hellas with liberty, here we lie, enjoying ageless glory.

and on the official memorial were inscribed these words:

This altar the Greeks erected to our Zeus of Freedom, the god of a free Greece, after their triumph drove the Persians away.

He outlined no political theory, but implied one when he declared that "the community is the teacher of men." He also praised the responsible citizen "in hands and feet and mind four-square and without a flaw . . . who freely chooses to do nothing harmful . . . the healthy man who knows how important a thing is justice within his city."

The defeat of Persia was essentially a democratic victory. It was common men of Athens who led the way in removing the threat of slavery from all Greece. Among the other Greek states there were a few which considered resistance against such a formidable enemy as the Persian Empire to be hopeless, and were ready to accept the best terms they could get; and even the oracle at Delphi advised the Athenians not to resist. In Athens itself some of the wealthier people, fearing democratic control by their fellow citizens more than foreign domination, were pro-Persian. But men who had come to realize the obligations as well as the privileges of liberty, led by a democrat whose courage was matched by his intelligence, refused to yield to despair; when their country was invaded and devastated by the Persians they fought all the harder; and the victory which they won justified their faith in themselves and guaranteed for their children the opportunity to build a greater commonwealth.

PART TWO

Athens:
Democracy and Empire

4

P E R I C L E S ' P L A T F O R M

For over thirty years, until his death in 429 B.C., another aristocrat by birth threw in his lot with the cause of the people and was the leader of the Athenian democracy. Pericles held no office except that of Strategos (General), but exercised his powerful influence in the determination of policy by his leadership in the assembly. What was his conception of the aims of Athens? Before analyzing how the democratic institutions actually worked, it will be interesting to see how Pericles wanted them to work. The best statement is given in the speech reported by

Thucydides, which was delivered on the occasion of the burial of the soldiers who had died for their country during the first year of the Peloponnesian War.

After a modest disclaimer of his ability to do justice to those who had made this sacrifice, for "acts deserve acts, not words of praise, in their honor," Pericles paid tribute to their forefathers and their contemporaries who had built up the state which now flourished. Then he proceeded to describe the sort of training which produced them and the political institutions and way of life which created this greatness.

> Our government [he said] is called a democracy, because its administration is in the hands, not of the few, but of the many. Yet, although all men are equal in the sight of the law, they are rewarded by the community on the basis of their merit; neither social position nor wealth, but ability alone, determines the service that a man renders. As we are liberally minded in our public life, so in our personal relations with one another we are generous; for we are not resentful nor do we look with disapproval when our neighbor enjoys himself in his own way, but are friendly and tolerant. In public matters we acknowledge the restraint of reverence, we are obedient to those who are in authority and to the laws, especially those laws which protect the less privileged and those unwritten ones whose transgression is admittedly shameful.
>
> But our city goes further than this. We have provided education and recreation for the spirit: athletic and religious festivals throughout the year,

and beauty in our public buildings, which delight our hearts day by day and banish sadness.

Our city is so great that the products of all the world flow into it, and we are happy in enjoying the fruits of other lands as well as of our own.

In our military policy we are similarly outstanding. We open our city to all the world, and never exclude any one from observing even what might be useful to him in a military way; for in an emergency we rely less on material devices than on our native courage. Our education also differs from that of our enemies. From childhood they laboriously discipline themselves in courage; but we, enjoying freedom, are none the less ready to face any danger when it comes. If, then, we choose to face peril with a liberated mind rather than after rigorous discipline, depending on courage which develops from our whole manner of life instead of state-made compulsion, the gain is ours: we avoid facing troubles until they come, and when they do come we meet them as bravely as our painfully toiling rivals.

We love beauty without extravagance and wisdom without weakness of will. Wealth we regard as an opportunity for public service rather than a cause for boasting, and poverty as not a shameful thing to acknowledge but a disgrace only if one does not try to overcome it. Our citizens are interested in both private and public affairs; concern over personal matters does not keep them from devoting themselves also to the community. In fact we regard the man who does no public service, not as one who minds his own business, but as worthless. All of us share in considering and deciding public policy, in the belief that debate is no hindrance to action, but that action is sure to fail when it is undertaken without full preliminary discussion. Consequently we show the utmost initiative in what we do and the utmost deliberation in what we plan. Other people are bold through ignorance, and hesitate when they stop to reflect, but those must rightly be regarded as most courageous who realize clearly what they face, yet do not shrink from danger. In our attitude toward neighboring states we are most generous, for we acquire friends, not by receiving favors, but by conferring them, with no self-interest in mind but in a spirit of confident liberality.

To sum it up, I claim that our city is an education to all Greece, and that every man among us is an example of independence of mind, versatility of accomplishment, and richly developed personality.[1]

Pericles went on to say that it was to save such a city and such a way of life that these soldiers died, and he pointed out the lesson for those who survived, that they, too, with so much at stake, must emulate the dead in sacrificing their own interests to the welfare of the city.

You must prove how precious such a spirit of devotion is, not by listening to the praise of heroes, but by daily appreciating the city's greatness, by falling in love with her as you see her, by realizing that her greatness is due to men of courage who know their duty and discipline themselves in its performance. Judging freedom to be happiness, and courage to be the creator of freedom, it remains for you not to fear any risks, but to rival what these men have done.[2]

So, he concluded, there is no reason to commiserate with the parents of the dead; life is hazardous at best, but they have known happiness and now know a noble sorrow. If possible they must have more children to serve and protect the city; and those who have families may be expected to work and plan most seriously since they have a greater stake in the welfare of the commonwealth. He added a word to the bereaved women, giving them advice which seems cold comfort: "Great is your glory if you do not lower your womanly nature and if men do not talk about you either in praise or blame." Finally he announced that the city would bring up the children of the dead at public expense.

This speech must, of course, be regarded partly as war propaganda, and it doubtless pictures a city more ideal than real; but in any event it describes the sort of city that Athenians would be willing to work and to die for. Is it a genuine democracy?

Judging by the assumptions outlined in the Introduction we must conclude that it is, in many respects. A large measure of personal freedom is granted each individual; the welfare of the entire community is the major interest of the city; the considered judgment of the people, based on free and full discussion, creates its policies; all abilities are utilized, the contribution of each enriching the happiness of all; the citizens feel that they have a stake in this society, which offers them so much and limits them so little, and are united in devotion to the political, economic, and cultural mission of Athens. With regard to foreign policy Pericles failed to take a correspondingly democratic attitude; he regarded Athens, not as a collaborator with her neighbors, but rather as their beneficent teacher and charitable superior.

If the picture drawn by Pericles were a true one of the Athens of his day, we might without hesitation acclaim the city as an admirable realization of democratic ideals. How true it was we shall proceed to investigate.

But there is one other question which should be answered first. In the history of democracies it is perhaps without parallel for one man to have exercised continuous leadership for so long a time. What was the secret of Pericles' influence with the Athenian people?

From the account given by Thucydides and Plutarch, and to a lesser extent by various other writers, it would appear that with two exceptions, the persuasiveness of his golden voice and his measures to provide work, pay and play for the people, he was not the typical democratic politician. His best friends were intellectuals and artists, such as Anaxagoras the physicist, Damonides the music critic, and Phidias the sculptor. He married a foreigner, Aspasia, regarding whom there was constant gossip of a most unfavorable sort, doubtless encouraged by the aristocratic cliques. In him there was an unusual combination of aloofness and gentleness in dealing with his associates. Yet he exerted such influence that Thucydides declared that under him Athens, a city famous for its shifting tides of public opinion, "although in name a democracy was virtually a government by its greatest citizen."

Regardless of their personal attitude toward him, the people could not be unaware of the value of his positive program. "Adequate pay for public service" was a plank in his platform which made it possible for even the poorest citizen to participate in state office. By providing festival grants, Plutarch says, "he amused the people like children, with far from vulgar pleasures." He created opportunities for those who were idle at home to become more effective as colonists abroad. Most important of all was his great program of public works, which he justified on the ground that it would glorify the city and, in the process, put the money of the city at the service of the people who needed it most and provide a great variety of jobs suited to their talents. Plutarch bears witness to the enthusiasm generated among the workers by this program, which liberated the energies of all sorts of craftsmen and resulted in buildings many of which stand today as evidence of the "everlasting glory" that Pericles envisaged.

Although he was thoroughly committed to the foreign policy of the democracy: expansion and the military protection of markets to increase Athenian trade and industry, even at the cost of war, his course as he continued in power became tempered with prudence; he did not advocate alarming risks, and often opposed what seemed to him adventures which promised gains beyond the capacity of the city to consolidate. Pleading for patience he once said, "If you will not listen to me, you will be wise to heed that wisest of all advisers, Time." And yet, with all his conciliatory tactics, on certain points he was adamant. He made no concessions to the aristocrats when they opposed imperialistic expansion and favored appeasement with oligarchical Sparta, or when they bitterly opposed his public-works program, charging that he "played fast and loose with public funds." He likewise restrained the radical democratic elements which thought the pace of spending and expansion was too slow. There was little for him to fear directly from the aristocrats, but at times popular resentment flared into opposition that was dangerous to his policies and to him personally. The people criticized him for marrying Aspasia; probably duped by aristocrats who wished to embarrass Pericles they forced the banishment of his best friends, Anaxagoras, Damonides and Phidias, and at one time fined him and deprived him of his generalship. But for the most part his leadership was acceptable to them; they were charmed by his eloquence and they had confidence in his ability.

The way in which he dealt with opposition is shown clearly in the speeches on war policy reported by Thucydides. Pericles believed that negotiation with Sparta was impossible, that if Athens yielded on any important point Sparta would mercilessly press her advantage. He accepted—even welcomed—the war as inevitable, and had no doubt that it could be won by maintaining control of the sea and fighting a defensive war on land. "We must not lament the loss of our houses and farms," he declared, "the important thing is to save our men." So he brought the farmers inside the city walls while the Athenian fleet guarded the empire and harassed the enemy. The farmers became indignant when they saw their fields and homes being ravaged; at one time Pericles flatly refused to call a meeting of the assembly until they quieted down. After the second invasion of Attica Pericles faced a still more discontented people, which began to blame him for starting the war and demanded negotiation with Sparta. He minced no words in dealing with this demand.

> I expected this [he said], once you began to feel the personal sufferings that war brings. But the welfare of the country must be set above any personal fortunes. Even though a man prospers in his business, yet if his country is ruined he perishes with it; but if his personal fortune is lost but his country is preserved he will in the long run be better off. War is a bad thing; but to submit to the dictation of other states is worse. Remember that you are citizens of a great city, enjoying institutions worthy of her greatness, and that their preservation is the best guarantee of your prosperity. Freedom, if we hold fast to it, will ultimately restore our losses, but submission will mean permanent loss of all that we value.[3]

He concluded: "To those of you who call yourselves men of peace, I say: You are not safe unless you have men of action at your side."

One unavoidable miscalculation of Pericles, however, had the most far-reaching consequences. The crowding of people inside the walls of Athens resulted in a plague which swept the city, wiping out a third of the population, causing Pericles' own death, and producing a radical change in the temper of those who survived. This one event was responsible to a large degree for the disasters which came to Athens in the course of the war. The loss of her first citizen was a crushing blow, the more so because too great reliance on a single leader had resulted in the failure to train others able adequately to take his place. No other statesman was so effective in reconciling the interests of the mercantile and laboring classes, on the coalition of which the liberal democracy was based. And the sound judgment of the people was badly shaken by the panic and widespread lawlessness that followed this hideous attack by an enemy against whom they were powerless.

Thucydides sums up the character of Pericles in glowing words: everyone recognized his ability and his honesty; "he restrained the multitude while at the same time respecting their liberties"; no flatterer, willing even to provoke the wrath of the people, he retained their confidence because of his measured judgment, liberal policies, and personal integrity. There is no reason for us to question his integrity, but whether his judgment and policies with regard to foreign affairs were as sound as Thucydides thought will require further consideration.

5

THE ATHENIAN

DEMOCRACY

Our government is called a democracy, because its administration is in the hands, not of the few, but of the
many. Whom did Pericles mean by "the many," and how
did they administer affairs?

First it must be understood that "the many" was a
relative term; it did not include a majority of the population. Political rights were enjoyed only by men over
eighteen years of age, born of Athenian parents enrolled
in the citizen class. This number in 430 B.C. was around
40,000. There were probably about 24,000 metics (resi-

dent aliens) who had settled in Athens for business, industrial, or professional purposes. If we add to these the women and children and upwards of 100,000 slaves (war-captives), who likewise had no part in public administration, it will appear that perhaps one-tenth of the total population had political rights. The reason for the restriction was the desire to have the policies of the city decided by those who had knowledge based on experience and a permanent stake in its welfare. But this certainly seems to be a decidedly limited democracy.

The electorate itself, however, was a thoroughly democratic group, including country gentlemen, business men, craftsmen, farmers and day laborers, of whom the last three classes formed a large majority. And these men actually did participate in government to a degree unknown in societies where a much larger proportion has been able to vote. Every policy, domestic or foreign, was formulated by the assembly, in the deliberations and decisions of which every citizen shared. The Council of Five Hundred, of which fifty members held active office each month, was the chief executive body, preparing the agenda for the assembly and overseeing financial and foreign affairs; this council was elected annually by lot from the roster of citizens over thirty years of age. Nearly all legal cases were tried in popular courts, for which there was a panel of six thousand citizens chosen annually by lot. It is clear that the legislative, executive and judicial functions of Athens were in the hands of all the citizens; there was representation in the executive and judicial bodies, to be sure, but on the extreme democratic principle of annual selection by lot. The same method of selection applied to the lesser administrative offices, including the Commissioners for Public Works, the Police Commissioners, and the Archons, who had charge of formal state occasions and presided over the law courts. There were no appointive offices, and only in the case of the Board of Generals did the people actually elect their representatives rather than choose them by lot, the principle being that military and naval strategy was a highly technical job which could not wisely be entrusted to any person whose lot might be drawn.

In practical terms this meant that every citizen of Athens during the course of his life had been engaged in public service. He had military training during the ages of eighteen to twenty; he listened in assembly to the debates, perhaps spoke himself, and shared in the decisions regarding governmental policy; he would probably have served on juries, which decided matters of civil law with no judges to instruct them; and he would likely have been on various commissions and a member of the Council of Five Hundred; perhaps on one day he was actually chairman of the Council (for that office, too, was passed around in a democratic way), so was virtually president of the Athenian Commonwealth.

It is obvious, therefore, that the ordinary citizen in Athens had an extraordinary opportunity for participating in political life; freedom to him meant, not so much the lack of restraint as the privilege of sharing in community enterprises. In fact it has been estimated that on any given day one citizen out of every four or five was engaged in some form of public service. As a result there was an extremely well informed and experienced citizenry. Such public activity was itself a liberal education. Bills before the assembly were of every conceivable sort. The city assumed many of the social services which we associate today with progressive government: ownership of such utilities as forests and mines; a program of public works and financial assistance to the distressed; the direction of religious, athletic, musical and dramatic festivals. Their management involved a large range of knowledge and interest on the part of the people who controlled them.

The poorer class could not afford to take time from their work regularly for such duties unless they received pay; hence the great importance of Pericles' legislation to extend pay to jurors as well as members of the Council. At the beginning of the fourth century pay was given also for attendance at the assembly.

The system of selection by lot of course favored the lower economic classes, who were in the majority, but it also guaranteed the representation of minorities. No "opposition" could be denied office by a dominant party. Thus the abilities of all elements were made available. In the election of generals the people likewise refused to draw rigid party lines. One of the most striking phenomena in Athenian politics is the fact that this important administrative office was entrusted to members of the leading conservativ. families, such as Miltiades, Cimon, Nicias and Alcibiades. If they had ability which could be used in the service of the people, under responsibility to the people, it was called upon.

With so many men constantly deciding public policies it might seem dangerous to have no check on their immediate expression of will. There was, in fact, the restraining influence of religious and social custom, which played a stabilizing rôle in all Greek life. There was the check of traditional procedures, which could be changed only by a court specially chosen to revise them. There were certain permanent laws guaranteeing basic personal rights; for instance, no citizen could be subjected to slavery or arrested for debt; a man charged with having committed a crime in company with others was given a separate trial, with complete freedom to present his case, and his punishment would not apply to members of his family. Action by the assembly was somewhat limited by the fact that the Council prepared the agenda. Furthermore, any citizen was free to challenge a decree passed by the assembly; then the mover of the legislation had to submit to judicial trial, and if he was convicted the decree was annulled. But it is nevertheless true that the assembly was by and large the sovereign body in Athens.

Similar confidence in the judgment of the entire citizenry appears in the legal system. Popular juries, sometimes as large as five hundred, uninstructed by judges, heard the plaintiff and defendant present their own cases, then gave their verdict by majority vote. Again the theory is soundly democratic: that justice can be determined best by the combined judgment of ordinary men, without distinctions of class or specialized training. The same principle governs our trial by jury, but the Athenians carried it even further by dispensing with judges.

Officials serving on various minor administrative commissions were closely watched by the people and were subject to frequent investigation. Every month a committee of the Council audited their accounts and certified whether they should be retained in office; their record was reviewed at the end of their term; and charges brought against them by any citizen were given prompt and thorough attention. Obviously the Athenians were realistic in not placing too great confidence in the honesty of any public official. A further check was the selection by lot for annual terms, which discouraged corruption and the building up of political machines.

We may properly ask how public policies or legal decisions could have been wisely made, or administration have been expertly performed, with such a lack of professional preparation and failure to focus responsibility. One answer is that the lack was not so great as would at first appear. These citizens were well educated as legislators, jurors, and administrators, by practical experience; if not, strictly speaking, specialists, they were by no means simply amateurs. Another answer is that if they failed to have the virtues of specialization they also avoided its vices; common sense would not tolerate the delays and technicalities that more professional legislative and judicial bodies are sometimes afflicted with. No satisfactory theoretical answer can be found for the failure to focus responsibility. It sometimes happened that the assembly voted a measure sponsored by any persuasive speaker, then entrusted its execution to men who had no belief in the wisdom of the policy. When it failed, who was to blame? Executives had responsibility for specific action only in so far as the assembly ordered it, and they could hardly be expected to promote earnestly what they had no share in initiating and disapproved of; and the assembly, varying from meeting to meeting according to the number present, could disown any previous decision. The original sponsor had, of course, no position of responsibility. That there were difficulties under this system in getting consistent policy-making must be granted.

But the most conclusive answer is the fact that this sort of government actually directed the city-state of Athens during the hundred years of its greatest development, creating within the city a culture of the first order, and controlling for more than half a century its political, economic and legal relations with approximately two hundred and fifty states included within the Athenian Empire. This is no mean achievement for any society; and especially for the first democracy which controlled an empire it is a political triumph.

We may conclude, then, that Athens denied political rights to important groups of its residents, but that the large number who did possess them enjoyed unusually active and significant political experience.

Men are rewarded by the community on the basis of their merit; neither social position nor wealth, but ability alone, determines the service that a man renders. Such was Pericles' claim. Was it justified as far as economic opportunity in Athens was concerned? Were men free from want? Were jobs available for them in accordance with their ability? Were the rewards on the basis of service rendered?

Here again we must note first of all the division of the population of Athens into three classes: citizens, metics, and slaves. Between citizens and metics there was no distinction regarding the kind of work that could be done or the rewards to be gained; the metics, having come to Athens to make a living, were chiefly business and professional men and highly skilled craftsmen who found work to their liking and satisfactory profits. But the slaves were obviously on a different footing. In so far as they were denied economic rights Athens was not democratic. We shall have to examine their status carefully.

Before we do this, however, one general observation should be made. Private economic interests, regardless of the status of the person concerned, were regarded and treated as subordinate to the general welfare. A striking instance of this attitude was a suit brought against members of the Corndealers' Guild who had bought up large quantities of grain in order to raise the price. Death was the penalty demanded by the prosecutor as fitting for such public enemies. Business, far from controlling government, was to a large extent conducted by metics who were not even allowed to vote. The state also recognized the obligation to give all its residents economic safeguards. It established export and import duties to provide adequate food at a reasonable price; it distributed food when necessary to the poor and disabled; it took money from the wealthy to finance the navy and the public festivals; it provided works projects to assure every man who had no private job a chance to labor for a living wage. There was in consequence no important problem of unemployment. The standard of living was not high, but people found it adequate. Stability was sought more than rapid improvement in economic conditions; the Athenians considered it possible to live well without being too comfortable.

It may be argued, however, that slaves had no share in this economic security. This assumption, so frequently made, is a dangerously facile one; "slavery" is a word which means little until the actual circumstances of living are understood. How did the slaves live? What economic satisfaction did they have? Were they simply the property of their masters, doing the servile work that no free man would do, regarded as chattels instead of persons? The answer to these questions is a crucial one for the purposes of this study of democracy, for it has often been claimed that the entire basis of Athenian civilization was slave labor which permitted the citizens freedom from manual work to engage in political and cultural activity.

Now it is obvious, since fully half of the citizens of

Athens were in the lowest economic order of workers, that slave labor did not provide such freedom from manual work for most of the citizens. Slave labor was a factor in the Athenian economy, useful because it increased the production of goods at low cost; but it was certainly not the basis of the Athenian way of life.

And when we examine living conditions among the slaves we find a different picture from that usually associated with the word "slavery." Perhaps one-fifth of the slaves, those whose abilities were mainly physical, were assigned to the mines, where their life was unquestionably a hard and short one. They were slaves in the worst sense of the word. (It may be questioned, however, whether mine-workers in any place or period, at least until very recent times, have been allowed to live a life worthy of free men, regardless of their political status.) But the rest had many economic advantages. Those who were bought from the city by individuals were protected from bodily harm by legislation; domestic slaves were treated as servants, often with affection and respect; those who worked as artisans and in business had their initiative and pride in their work encouraged by being paid wages, which they could save and with which in many cases they ultimately bought their freedom. And a great number of slaves remained the property of the state; they had freedom of residence and conditions of living, simply reporting for the work to which they were assigned; they, too, received pay and in time could purchase their freedom. It was to the interest of individual owners and the state that these slaves should be employed in work that they could do best and under conditions which would lead them to work well. From fifth-century records of state labor projects we get the revealing testimony that slaves worked side by side with citizens and metics in both unskilled and highly skilled jobs, and that occasionally a slave was even foreman of a project. On this same basis of responsibility slaves were used for other state services: they were the policemen of Athens, and minor officials such as clerks and inspectors of weights and measures.

What can we conclude from this? That even slaves had many of the essential economic freedoms: the opportunity to do respectable work which they were capable of doing and enjoyed doing, under living conditions which gave them a large amount of personal freedom, a living wage, and even the prospect of eventual complete personal liberty. The picture must not, of course, be too brightly drawn; these people could not escape the feeling that they were the property of some one else; many of them were treated cruelly, all of them were underpaid, and even when they gained personal liberty they had no political rights. Slavery, at its best, is intolerable in a democracy. But from an economic point of view there is no doubt that very many Greek slaves had security and achieved happiness. The best proof is the fact that until 103 B.C. there were no slave revolts of any magnitude in Athens.

Furthermore, because of this mixing of free and slave

labor on the democratic basis of ability for the job, there developed very little class distinction between slaves and "poor whites." The slaves were often expert craftsmen and business men, whose work was an education to the free Athenians beside whom they labored and with whom they associated. The result was increased efficiency on the part of the citizens, and productive competition based on the recognition of merit wherever it might be found.

After a thorough examination of all the evidence, Alfred E. Zimmern and William L. Westermann have appraised the Athenian slave system. According to Professor Westermann, "In any sense which implies either that the enslaved population predominated over the free or that the Greek city-states displayed the mentality of a slave-ridden society, Greek culture was not founded upon slavery." [1] Professor Zimmern goes farther; his judgment is that "Greek society was not a slave-society; but it contained a sediment of slaves to perform its most degrading tasks, while the main body of its so-called slaves consisted of apprentices haled in from outside to assist, together and almost on equal terms with their masters, in creating the material basis of a civilization in which they were hereafter to share." [2] "Almost on equal terms with their masters" must be judged an exaggeration, but the verdict is generally a sound one.

"In which they were hereafter to share." Here we come to the essential democracy of Athens—its approximation to social equality. Class distinctions were not abolished, but they were minimized; Pericles was true to the facts when he declared, *In our personal relations with one an-other we are generous.* It was a complaint of the aristo-crats that in dress and manner the slaves were indistin-guishable from the rest of the citizens; and in the fourth century Demosthenes declared that "many slaves in Athens enjoy greater freedom of speech than the citizens of some other states." The evidence indicates that nearly all men residing in Athens had a real share in the life of the city and enjoyed its cultural opportunities, the "edu-cation and recreation for the spirit" of which Pericles boasted.

One final (and important) reservation must be made. We have already noted that this democratic conception did not include women. Athenian life was essentially masculine; even the wives of citizens took no part in public affairs, their place was considered to be the home. There they, too, had security, the responsibility of man-aging household affairs and educating the younger chil-dren. But the restrictions on their freedom were many. Girls had their husbands chosen for them by their par-ents; if they later went through the difficult procedure of securing a divorce they still had to have a male guardian who took care of their money, and the children were given to the husband; their social activities were chiefly with women friends. Xenophon indicated the prevailing attitude toward them when he named the qualifications for a good wife as "habits of temperance, modesty, and teachableness." The metic women, companions of Athenian men, had more social freedom than the wives;

slave women had many of the privileges of trusted domestic servants, but were of course subject to dictation by their masters.

These political, economic and social institutions, many of them democratic in character, some of them far from democratic, produced the culture of fifth-century Athens. It may reasonably be argued that a still greater civilization might have resulted from a wider distribution of responsibility, with the abilities of women, aliens and slaves fully utilized and their devotion to the common welfare quickened by the consciousness of participation in the complete life of the city. But, in any event, no group of leisurely aristocrats should receive credit for the drama, the festivals, the fine arts, the speculation regarding human values, the zest for living, which flourished then as in few other periods of history. It was, instead, almost the entire community of men, working together on a basis of unusually equal opportunity, which created and controlled that culture.

6

EMPIRE

To the domestic problems facing fifth-century Athens were added the more complicated ones of a democracy controlling an empire.

The empire grew out of the Delian League, a confederation of over two hundred states chiefly on the islands and the coast of Asia Minor, which was organized following the defeat of Persia to guarantee future security against that threat. The sacred island of Delos was the headquarters of the league, the seat of the Council in which every member had an equal vote, the law courts which were to settle disputes arising among members, and the treasury. Aristides ("The Just") of Athens was chosen to prepare an annual budget, based on ability to pay, for the purpose of building and operating ships for naval protection and for administering the other functions of the league.

It is interesting to follow the stages whereby this league of free states became the Athenian Empire. The underlying reason was that Athens had naval resources which far outstripped those of any other state; consequently most of the ships were built in Athenian yards and were manned by Athenian sailors. The league from the start was dominated by Athens; her superior power led to her controlling the votes of the smaller states in the Council, and the officials who collected and administered the revenue were all Athenians. Soon the treasury was transferred to Athens, and Athenian courts supplanted those of the league. Since the chief city was involved far more than any other in the expenditure of funds and the legal cases which arose, it seemed expedient to effect these changes.

Thucydides traced with unerring skill the transformation from the league into the empire. There were three motives involved in its development, he declared. The first was the fear of Persia, which originally bound the states together, but which became less operative as the danger diminished. It was succeeded by Athens' sense of honor in being the capital city. The funds of the league were now in Athens, steadily increasing and far surpassing what was needed for purposes of defense. What could be more natural than to use them for the glorification of the league's center of culture? It was partly from this source that Pericles financed his program of public works, justifying the action, in spite of bitter protests from the allies, on the ground that Athens was providing protection for the states that furnished the money and should therefore use the funds as it saw fit. This "honorable mission" of Athens was obviously a far cry from the idea of a confederation of sovereign states. Yet Athens was by no means an oppressive master. The record shows that her courts were scrupulously fair in judging commercial cases; the allies kept their local autonomy as long as they had democratic governments satisfactory to Athens; and save for the tribute money which they paid they were not financially exploited.

Both the excellence and the weakness of Athenian imperial policy were revealed in the handling of legal cases involving members of the league. As far as commercial suits were concerned there was no just cause for complaint; the allies were dealt with on a treaty basis of reciprocity, with safeguards provided for means of redress in case there was any violation of treaty obligations. Regardless of Athens' motives in making this arrangement—honest dealing was obviously in the interest of her trade —the allies received fair treatment. But political and criminal cases were a different matter. All cases involving Athenians were, of course, tried in Athens; but even when only citizens of allied states were concerned, appeal from a verdict of death, exile or loss of civil rights could be made to an Athenian court. And although Athens claimed that there was no legal discrimination against the allies, the charge of Aristophanes that she treated them shamefully seems somewhat justified by the facts. For a citizen of an allied state to come to Athens for trial meant inconvenience and expense; frequently there was a long delay before the case was decided; and there can be no question that a democrat was likely to fare better at the hands of an Athenian jury than an aristocrat. It is also possible that some Athenian officials made money by giving special consideration to litigants who were willing to pay for it. Here was a legitimate cause of allied resentment. Athens would have been wiser if she had extended her liberal policy regarding commercial cases to the political and criminal ones as well, and wiser still if she had led the way in establishing a system of courts which included other members of the league.

Athens furnished her allies protection; but she did much better by herself in protecting and extending her trade routes to the northeast. Her commerce came to dominate the entire Aegean and the Black Sea area. This was, of course, to the interest of the commercial and industrial workers in Athens, so the foreign policy of the democratic majority was definitely expansionist and imperialistic.

Gradually resentment against the increasing power of Athens grew among her traditional enemies, especially the great commercial city of Corinth, whose trade was being steadily throttled. The outcome of this resentment, which Athens fanned rather than attempted to mitigate, was the Peloponnesian War, in which a coalition of Sparta, Corinth and Thebes raised the slogan of freeing Hellas from a tyrant city—ironical indeed, since Sparta was an oligarchy which remained in power only by the most brutal oppression, while Athens claimed to be an education to all Greece in the liberal way of life. But there was justice in the charge. Athens, democratic in domestic policy, had never attempted to organize her empire on a similar basis; she regarded her allies as inferior states.

The third motive which caused the empire, says Thucydides, was self-interest. This showed in all its ugliness when the allies began to grow restive and revolt was in the air. If this were really the Delian League there was no reason why a member should not withdraw. But of course it was no longer such a league. Athens by this time could not afford to give up either the military or the financial advantages she got from her subject states. A critical test came when the wealthy and strategic city of Mitylene attempted to break away from the league in 428 B.C., only about a year after Pericles' death. Athens promptly blockaded the island and starved it into submission, then debated what punishment should be meted out to these "rebels." Should it be execution of the oligarchical ringleaders, or death for all the men and slavery for the women and children? The assembly, holding that a severe lesson should be made of Mitylene in order to impress the other subject states, at first voted the latter penalty, but then reopened the question for debate. Thucydides has recorded the gist of the arguments with which Cleon, Pericles' successor as popular leader, advocated the severest penalty, and Diodotus, a more liberal democrat, urged on grounds of expediency a milder one. Their arguments show how radically the Athenian temper had changed even in this short time as a result of war, the plague, and the sense of national danger.

> I have often realized [Cleon said] that a democracy is incompetent to control an empire, but never more than today, when I see you having a change of heart about the people of Mitylene. In your daily relations with one another you have no fear or suspicion, so you regard your allies in the same way, forgetting that when they win you over to pity you fall into danger and they feel no gratitude. You must remember that your empire is a despotism imposed on intriguing subjects who are ruled against their will, who obey you, not because of any kindness you do them or any good will they feel toward you, but only in so far as you are stronger than they are and impose your will on them. But the most important thing of all is that we stop everlastingly changing our minds, and realize that a state with inferior laws which are enforced is better off than one whose laws are good but ineffective.[1]

Cleon went on to charge the Athenians with being captivated by clever speakers, eager to listen to every new idea, whereas the immediate problem was actually a simple one to be settled by the common sense of realistic minds. Mitylene had revolted, although Athens always treated it generously and gave it no justification for revolt; if such conspiracy and rebellion were not punished promptly and severely the whole foundation of the empire would be undermined. With an odd perversion of words Cleon argued that Mitylene really attacked Athens, waiting to stab her until she was engaged with enemies. That was insolent action, said Cleon, and for it all the people of Mitylene should pay the price, as an example to the people in other subject states not to trust in their might against the right of Athens!

So I maintain that you should not reverse your former decision or be misled by pity, delight in clever arguments, or mercy—those three things most prejudicial to empire. Mercy should be reserved for those who will show mercy, not for those who are necessarily our enemies. I will sum it all up in one word: If you take my advice you will do what is both just to the people of Mitylene and what is expedient for us; but if you decide otherwise you will not be thanked by them but rather condemned: for if these people had a right to revolt, then you are wrong in exercising imperial power. But if, rightly or wrongly, you are resolved to rule, then you must punish these people, justly or not, in your own interest. If you don't, you must give up your empire, and then you can practise your virtues to your hearts' content. I say punish them as we formerly decided. Pay them back for the trouble they have caused. Stop being tenderhearted, remember the danger that we lately faced, and by punishing them warn your other allies that whoever revolts shall perish. If they realize that, you will not be forced to neglect your enemies to fight against your own allies.[2]

To this speech, brutally frank in its appeal to motives of self-interest, Diodotus replied with one milder in tone, but with no greater concern for justice. He urged the assembly to avoid haste, passion and impulsiveness; argument is a guide to wise action, he declared, and those who warn men to distrust it are either stupid or have private ends of their own to serve. The question, he said, is not one of justice, of right or wrong, but simply of expediency: what action will be most profitable. If killing all these men will keep our other subjects from revolting, kill them; but it may be that such an exhibition of brutality will have the opposite effect; men always hope to succeed, and they will struggle all the harder if they realize that they must either win or be utterly wiped out. Athenian policy should be to watch her allies closely so as to keep them from starting a revolt, but if a revolt does occur it is wiser to deal with it as if it were caused by a small faction, so that the majority of the people among the allies will be disposed to be friendly.

In this case the assembly followed the advice of Diodotus; only the ringleaders were killed. But the type of argument shows how foreign any conception of democracy was to the Athenians in their relations with other states in the so-called league.

In 416 B.C., another episode occurred which reveals still

more clearly the increasing autocracy of Athens' foreign policy. The small island of Melos, off the eastern coast of the Peloponnesus, had observed strict neutrality during fifteen years of war. But Athens finally decided it would be a useful base for naval operations, so she sent envoys to invite Melos to enter the "league." The Melians realized that the choice was between death in battle or slavery by submission. "Quite so," answered the Athenians.

> We won't use any fine phrases, saying that we have a right to our empire because we conquered the Persians, or that we are attacking you now because you have done us any harm. We both know well enough that justice is arrived at by deliberation only when the two sides are equal; and that the powerful exact what they can and the weak yield what they must.[3]

The Melians then tried to persuade the Athenians that it would be expedient for Athens to spare them, because Athens, if later conquered by Sparta, would suffer worse if she herself had set such an example of cruelty. "That's our risk," the Athenians curtly replied,

> but we are not worried. Major powers don't have to fear each other so much as they do the intrigues of their inferiors. It will be obviously expedient for you to keep on living, even if in submission, and for us to get you without sacrificing our men and materials.[4]

The Melians then asked why they could not remain neutral. "Because," the Athenians replied, "in the eyes of our subjects your neutrality would be a proof of our weakness, but your hatred is a proof of our power." Finally the Melians called upon the gods: "We trust in the gods, because we are god-fearing men defending themselves against men who are unjust." To this the Athenians cynically replied:

> We expect to have the favor of the gods quite as much as you, for of the gods we believe, as of men we know, that by a necessity of their nature they rule wherever they have the power. This is no principle invented by us, nor are we the first to act upon it; we found it already existing and expect all people after us to use it. You and others, if you had the power we have, would do what we are doing. So be sensible, and submit.[5]

But the Melians chose to die rather than submit and give up the liberty which their city had enjoyed for centuries. The Athenians defeated them handily, killed or enslaved them, then settled their own citizens on the island and thereafter used it in the campaigns against Sparta.

This growing attitude of arrogant ambition on the part of Athenian imperialism found its most spectacular effort—and failure—in the expedition against Syracuse the following year. The campaign, boldly conceived though it was and staking nearly everything on one throw of the dice, might have succeeded, virtually assuring

Athens of victory over the coalition of her enemies, had the command been unified and the execution swift and able. But after fifteen years of war Athens had come to mistrust her leadership, so she divided the responsibility, choosing as one of the generals a cautious conservative who lacked faith in the expedition from the start. It was foredoomed to tragic failure.

After this debacle, party strife increased in Athens; the morale of the city was weakened; there was increasing criticism of the ability of a democratic government successfully to prosecute the war, a more urgent demand from the aristocratic groups for an understanding with Sparta, a growth in personal and party ambition which swayed men more than patriotism. The most spectacular example of unscrupulous personal ambition was the brilliant but unprincipled opportunist, Alcibiades. The situation was not unique in Athens. All over the war-wracked Greek world revolution was brewing, as aristocrats and democrats, rich and poor, placed party above country and assailed each other more bitterly than they did the common enemy.

Thucydides, in the third book of his *History of the Peloponnesian War*, describes the pattern of these revolutions in unforgettable terms:

> Revolution wrought terrible calamities in the cities of Greece, such as have existed and always will exist as long as human nature remains as it is, but which change in character under varying conditions. In times of peace and prosperity states and individuals,

not subject to imperious necessity, are governed by higher motives; but war, taking away the comforts of life, is a hard master and molds men's characters to fit their circumstances.

As the revolutionary spirit grew in intensity, men surpassed their predecessors in the ingenuity of their plots and the brutality of their revenge. Words no longer meant what they had before, but were distorted to serve personal and party purposes: recklessness was called loyal courage; prudent delay, cowardice; restraint, weakness of will; frantic energy, true manliness. The ties of party were stronger than those of family, because a partisan would act without daring to ask why. No agreements were binding if there was an opportunity of breaking them successfully. For party associations, it should be understood, are not based on law nor do they seek the common welfare; they are lawless and seek only self-interest.

The cause of all these evils was greed, ambition, and the love of power, and the party spirit which they created. Leaders of one faction would pretend to uphold the equality of the many, the other the superior wisdom of an aristocracy, whereas in reality both considered only what profit they could make for themselves at the expense of the people. They committed the most atrocious crimes with a complete disregard of any process of law. Religion meant nothing to either group, but it was cynically used in order to gain selfish ends. Those who belonged to neither party were the prey of both.

So revolution produced every kind of evil in Greece. In their feeling of insecurity men looked only to their own safety and trusted no one. Those of inferior minds were generally most successful, for they acted speedily and without scruples. The poor struck to seize their neighbors' property. Men who had personal grudges took their revenge with unbridled cruelty. While conditions of life were in complete disorder, people gave way to uncontrolled passions and disregarded those common laws of humanity in which every person normally trusts for his protection.[6]

Athens had an experience of this sort in 411 B.C., although not on as brutal a scale as some of the other states.

For a considerable time discontent with the strategy, or even the continuance, of the war had been growing. The aristocrats had, of course, been opposed from the start to the policy of imperial expansion and the war that resulted from it. But now they were joined by a much more powerful group of influential business men, some of whom believed that if the war was to continue they should have a greater voice in directing its policy, since they were bearing a large part of the burden of financing it, and others who had come to share the view of the aristocrats that a profitable peace could be made with Sparta. So the coalition of business men and workers which flourished under the leadership of Pericles was challenged by a new coalition of the old nobility and many prominent merchants, who plotted to get control of the government.

At first they dangled before the people the prospect of securing financial aid from Persia if a temporary oligarchical regime friendly to Persia should supplant the democracy, and they won some support from the war-weary citizens for this program. When Persia refused to play the game, plans had gone so far that they struck swiftly to get control, and by a skillful combination of murder, intimidation and fair promises prevailed upon the assembly to abdicate in their favor. Their ostensible program was to reorganize the government on a broad oligarchical basis, by limiting the franchise to men of some means and abolishing pay for nearly all state offices. But "for the emergency" a coalition council of four hundred members assumed complete legislative and executive powers. Moderates in the coalition, headed by Theramenes, expected that this would be supplanted soon by a somewhat more representative governing body, but the directing minds had no such desire; they planned to make the provisional government a permanent one. But it had a stormy time during its four months of control. Sparta refused to make peace, preferring to encourage dissension in Athens rather than to deal with any stable government. Then for a brief period Theramenes' group got the upper hand, and established a constitution based on the original program which took away political power from the lower economic classes. But this also lasted only a few months. When the imperial democratic navy returned to the city, the coalition was forced out of office and democracy was restored.

From this time, however, until the defeat of Athens in 404 B.C., the oligarchs continued to plot against the majority of the people. While Cleophon, the new democratic leader, worked to relieve the financial distress of the poor, partly by a dole, partly by resuming the public-works program, and while the weary sailors gallantly continued the struggle against Sparta, which was now being aided by Persia, the oligarchs intrigued. There is some reason to believe that their tactics included stirring up dissension and even treachery within the army. Their chance finally came when Athens was forced to acknowledge defeat. Then, supported by a Spartan garrison, a group known as the Thirty assumed control.

Theramenes again attempted to collaborate with them, vainly hoping for the restoration of a moderate conservative government; but when the Thirty started a reign of terror, brutally murdering some fifteen hundred of the leading democrats, he protested at the cost of his life.

The tradition of freedom in Athens was too strong to allow for long submission to oligarchic rule. This regime lasted only as long as the Spartan army remained; then the democrats fought their way back to power, and never lost control again until Athens came under the yoke of Macedon. Then, too, the set-back was a temporary one, in effect only as long as a Macedonian garrison enforced it. Regardless of reverses, Athens insisted on being a democracy.

A city bled white of men and resources by nearly thirty years of war, its empire smashed, its commercial system undermined, its prestige vanished, now faced the world as a shadow of its former self. As time went on there was a partial recovery. The economic structure was rebuilt, and Athens continued to be a center of art and education not only for Greece but also for the wider world, East and West, under Alexander the Great and Rome. But the city's dominant influence in Mediterranean politics was gone forever, and with it the spirit of confidence and enthusiasm which had formerly united the Athenians in the creation of a great culture.

A question which must be asked, although probably no satisfactory answer can be given, is this: how could the debacle have been avoided?

Military authorities explain that Athens could have won the war. Her prospects at the beginning were excellent, and if the plague had not smitten the city she might have achieved victory within a few years. Even after the plague a little more luck and better strategy on certain occasions would probably have turned the tide in her favor. But as the war dragged on there was such bitterness on both sides that it is highly improbable that any productive or lasting peace would have been made. Were there other policies that might have been more effective than the military one?

One answer was given by the aristocrats, who insisted that Athens should never have developed as an industrial and commercial state, or built up the empire which inevitably involved the city in war. If she had been content to remain a small provincial city, largely self-sufficient and friendly with Sparta, obviously she would not have needed to build up her markets, protect her trade routes, or create an empire. That was precisely the aristocratic aim for Athens: an agricultural community governed by country gentlemen. But we have no reason to believe that any such community would have created a great culture.

It may be argued that, although the political and cultural institutions of Athens were conditioned by its being an expanding commercial and industrial city, still the expansion might have continued at a less ambitious rate without the risks of imperial adventure; by gradual economic and cultural penetration Athens could have built up an enduring supremacy. If tribute money had not been available the progress would have been less rapid, but in the long run it would probably have been even more substantial. Unfortunately, however, it is not easy to curb such expansion or to decline an empire that is one's for the taking. In the convenient perspective of history we can say that Athens would have been wiser, no doubt, to remember her traditional aversion to pride and excess and her respect for moderation.

Again, granting the empire, was war inevitable? Could not Athens have avoided it by adopting a more conciliatory policy toward both her economic enemies and her "allies"? If the war had been avoided, the plague would not have occurred and Athenian human and material resources would have increased instead of being depleted. It is conceivable that the city might have built up a lasting empire. The possibility is an attractive one; but we must not forget how strong the spirit of independence in the small Greek cities was, or the jealousies which constantly arose, or the economic rivalry between Athens and Corinth which required a great deal more give and take to settle than either's ambition would permit, or the profound antipathy of Sparta. There does, however, seem reason to believe that Athens might have avoided the war if she had been willing to expand more gradually and show more regard for the feelings of her neighbors. The fact is, of course, that she did not want to do so because she was confident of winning the war.

Granting the empire, need it have continued on an autocratic basis? Athens succeeded in doing so much as a pioneer in democracy that it may be unfair to expect more of her; but the suggestion may be offered that her greatest mistake lay in not extending the principles of democratic self-government throughout her empire, transforming it into a Commonwealth of City-States. Even Pericles apparently never thought that possible; he spoke frankly of the empire as a tyranny. But it is conceivable that Athens could have created a genuine league of Greek states, in which the freedoms which she enjoyed, and even more enlightened ones, could have been projected to interstate relations. An inevitable handicap was the primitive system of communications, which must have hampered any democratic formulation of policy or concerted action on a large scale. A greater handicap, but not an inevitable one, was the limitation of Athenian democracy at home. No state which tolerated slavery could be expected to treat weaker states as equals. But if Athens, with her resources, experience, and imagination, had led such a movement, the chances of its success would have been far greater than those of the later reasonably effective attempts made by the Achaean League and other small confederations.

This is all, of course, in the realm of conjecture. What we know is that Athens reached a high degree of creative culture in her quite democratic society; and that she sacrificed much of it by constructing an empire on an autocratic basis and then being willing to risk war for even greater stakes.

7

COMMUNITY ART

*We have provided education and recreation for the spirit
. . . beauty in our public buildings, which delight our
hearts day by day and banish sadness . . . We love beauty
without extravagance.*

In these words Pericles gave an extraordinary reason
why men should gladly die for their country. It is probably the only instance in history of a statesman urging
his people to be patriotic because their state offered them
aesthetic opportunities. But the explanation is not far to
seek. In Athens the arts were regarded as a normal and

102

necessary expression of community life, created by and for the people. Artists were not looked upon as exotic members of society, producing for the cultured or wealthy few. Not many of them were even recognized as artists; they were artisans, men who did their daily work with stone and bronze and clay, and drew their pay for a job well done like any other craftsmen. Only the most distinguished, such as the sculptors Myron and Phidias and the architects Ictinus, Callicrates and Mnesicles, won any great name for themselves. Most of the art of the Periclean period was produced by ordinary workers, citizens, metics and slaves.

Not only were the objects of art created by ordinary men, but they were also the common property of ordinary men. The most important commissions were not given by wealthy patrons for sumptuous private homes and sculpture satisfying their personal taste, but by the city for public projects. Here was a democratic art. And its vitality and progress may fairly be attributed to the fact that it served community purposes and was constantly appraised by a population interested in it and sensitive to it.

Since artistic expression was so intimately linked with the whole of Athenian life, in the arts we find an invaluable record of the city's evolution during its greatest century. The subjects chosen for representation show where the people's interest lay; the aesthetic treatment reveals the quality of the public taste. By making a survey of characteristic fifth-century art, therefore, we may effectively supplement the historical and literary record. The evolution was, of course, much more complex than any brief summary can do justice to, but the main outlines will indicate how truly the art mirrored Athenian social development, and the variants bear witness to the fact that in this field also there was no sterile uniformity.

A study of the most modest of the arts, that of the vase-painters, will provide a useful frame of reference for the more substantial arts of architecture and sculpture.

In the last half of the sixth century Athenian pottery began to corner the market and secure a virtual monopoly throughout the Mediterranean world. The explanation is threefold: local clay deposits were of unusually fine quality, Pisistratus imported the best skilled craftsmen he could find, and expanding trade made it necessary to have a large number of containers as well as objects for export. This was one purpose served by Greek pottery. The so-called "vases" were made for practical use. There were jars for exporting oil and wine, as well as every kind of utensil for domestic kitchen, dining room, dressing room and ceremonial purposes. The extent to which Athenian trade dominated the Greek world during the fifth century has been demonstrated by the thousands of Athenian vases discovered in excavations on the shores of the Mediterranean and far inland.

The vase-paintings furnish us with a complete illustration of Athenian activities. Nearly every subject was pictured: home life in many phases, education, sports, worship, battles, representations of the gods and heroes.

No two pictures are alike; painters did original drawings for each vase, giving free rein to their individual imagination. Yet in certain technical respects there are similarities in trends, and a definite evolutionary pattern can be traced.

During the time of Pisistratus, Ionian influence was pronounced, finding expression in sensuous and sophisticated designs with figures wearing elaborate costumes gaily decorated with embroideries. When democracy came into its own at the turn of the century, there was a notable change in the character of the work; the shapes became more cleanly cut, the designs were charged with greater energy and dynamic power. In many ways this was the most exhilarating period of the potters' craftsmanship; the intensity of experience and the pioneering enthusiasm of Athens were reflected in the work of the painters. The best representative of this spirit was Brygus, a potter who had a flourishing business with several painters working under his direction. In his pictures, showing scenes from the gymnasia, battlefields and religious rites, but most of all blithe revels, we see the actual life of the times represented with zest and sensitiveness. The technique was likewise of a pioneering type, with crisp linear precision, nervous but crystal-clear compositions, and experiments in color contrasts and shaded edges. Even the less dynamic painters, among whom Hieron was outstanding, drew their figures with buoyant grace.

By the beginning of the Periclean period Athens had matured; the earlier verve and ambition were developing into calm confidence and well-disciplined power. This mood is seen in vase-paintings of the time. The figures are broader in scale and freer in rhythm, characterized by amplitude and dignity rather than brisk action. These painters made a synthesis of Doric strength and Ionic charm, to create a style distinctively Athenian. In the work of the Cleophrades painter, the Penthesilea painter and Polygnotus this tendency is especially marked. Other artists, still clinging to the Ionic tradition, abandoned the rather brittle linear treatment of their predecessors and painted decorative pieces with exquisite refinement. The great work of the mural painter Polygnotus has unfortunately not survived, but it is a fair assumption that his designs were similar in character, since they are doubtless reflected in the vase-paintings.

As life became more varied and less sure of itself in the last third of the century, there was a corresponding change in the vase-drawings. The pace was feverishly quickened, a multitude of accessories were introduced, design was sacrificed to realism, clarity submerged in complex scenes, wherein figures often covered the vase on various levels and bits of landscape were included to add further variety. We are told that the mural painter Zeuxis prided himself on such realistic devices; and on the vases of the Meidias painter and Aristophanes we see how the large, clearly spaced designs of the earlier time were replaced by picturesque detail. There is interesting illustration in these vases, but a lack of strength. A disintegrating individualism was well on its way.

The most ambitious art project of Athens was, of course, Pericles' building program. During the years 450–420 B.C., no less than six major temples, the entrance hall to the Acropolis, the Hall of Mysteries at Eleusis, and a music auditorium were constructed, and doubtless other buildings of which we have no record. The famous town-planning expert, Hippodamus, was brought from Miletus to design the expanding port city of the Piraeus on geometrical principles. Plutarch has given us a vivid picture of the spirit in which the people of Athens worked on these projects.

> The buildings arose, no less impressive in their grandeur than inimitable in their grace of form, since the workers were eager to outdo themselves in the beauty of their craftsmanship. Most amazing of all was the speed with which the buildings were completed; with regard to each one men thought that many generations would be required to complete it, yet all were finished during a single period. To this day they seem recently erected, so fresh is their vigor, so lasting their bloom, which keeps them unaffected by the touch of time, as though the ever-invigorating breath of an ageless spirit had been infused into them.[1]

The evolution of architecture followed a general pattern similar to that of the vase-paintings, from an early emphasis on spirited design, through a "strong" period, to increasing complexity and grace at the expense of firmly disciplined organization. In the middle of the century it also achieved a synthesis of Doric logic and Ionic decorative refinement. The Doric is a masculine style of vigorous mass, simple composition, logical relationships and functional construction; the Ionic is more feminine, emphasizing graceful contours and elaborate decoration. What the Athenians did was to make use of the best elements in both, producing a style which combined grace and strength.

This tendency is seen as early as the beginning of the fifth century in the Athenian Treasury at Delphi, a trim little structure in which the ponderous proportions of the native Doric were modified to suit the more cosmopolitan Athenian taste. The fact that it was erected at Delphi is evidence of the ambition of Athens to keep in favor with this international center as well as her satisfaction in commemorating her military victories at such a strategic place. The building was generously decorated with sculpture, representing the exploits of Heracles and Theseus, one the pioneer hero of all the Greeks, the other a hero belonging exclusively to Athens. It is significant that the episodes in which Theseus overcame public enemies were given the most prominent position and were modeled with the most sensitive feeling. The style is similar to that of contemporary vase-paintings, crisp designs of lithe forms built chiefly on diagonal lines that increase the nervous vitality of the compositions.

During the Periclean period the synthesis of Doric and Ionic was perfected. The best example is the Parthenon, the temple built in honor of Athena, guardian goddess of Athens. This is a massive building, about 650 feet in perimeter, with an imposing row of forty-six great Doric columns around it and a second row of columns in each porch. The first impression it gives is one of noble simplicity, dignity and power. But closer inspection reveals that the proportions were calculated with such delicate variations, and the refinements were so subtly designed, that it has lyrical charm as well as dramatic power. It avoids monotony by a complicated series of slightly curved lines and planes throughout, so that the effect is one of flexibility and resilience instead of mechanical regularity. The "style" was not a static one, taken from copybooks, but one which had developed out of the emotional and intellectual growth of the people. Here, we may say, is a building expressive of responsible men who lived and worked in the strength and variety of freedom.

Its sculpture was especially appropriate decoration from both a social and aesthetic point of view. Phidias' great ivory and gold statue of Athena in the interior was of course the most important single work, but since we can visualize it only in terms of the crude small adaptations which remain, there is no sound basis for critical judgment. But most of the decorative sculpture has survived; some of it is still on the building, most of the rest is now in the British Museum. It harmonizes perfectly with the architecture, having a similar breadth and dignity of mass, with great variety and charm in its subordinate details.

For the two pediments subjects were chosen which represent the divine protection of the city. On the east end the birth of Athena from the brain of Zeus was pictured, with heavenly messengers announcing the news to the gods and the legendary heroes of the city; in the corners were horses of the sun and moon, fixing the time of the divine birth. On the west pediment Athena and Poseidon were pictured in their contest for the lordship of Athens, which Athena won by vote of the citizens when she offered them the olive tree; on either side were Athenians judging the contest and local river gods in the corners to symbolize the setting. From an aesthetic point of view the massive forms mounted perfectly within the limiting lines of the triangle, and were intimately related to one another, not only by a fluent lateral rhythm, but also by being interwoven backward and forward within the field. Whether consciously or not, Phidias composed a design in three dimensions which repeated the structural modeling of the mountain background, harmonizing with the surroundings as well as the building. Similarly in the application of color to this as well as the other decorative sculpture, kinship was established with the brilliant blue sky and the purple hills of Athens.

The separate figures repay careful study as examples of Athenian sensitiveness. Among the best preserved are the so-called "Three Fates." We cannot identify them surely, but the most likely interpretation is that they represent Artemis, Aphrodite and Persuasion. Artemis, patron goddess of women, sits erect; the body of Aphrodite is more sensuous, as befits her nature as goddess of love; Persuasion rests against her, luxuriously reclining toward a corner. The three forms, massive and dignified, are none the less graceful; the drapery, kept subordinate so as not to detract from the mighty outlines of the bodies, performs a valuable function in unifying them; the folds lead persuasively from one form to the next and also curve inward around them. As a result of the oblique placing of the figures and the curvilinear inward rhythm the forms stand out strongly against their background. The total effect is one of noble power, combined with gracious vitality.

The metopes on the Parthenon represent various aspects of pride being punished: the gods overcoming presumptuous giants, Lapith heroes subduing drunken Centaurs, Greeks defeating Amazons and Trojans. These sturdy designs offer a much more interesting variety of patterns than those on the Athenian Treasury, including horizontal, vertical, oblique and circular compositions. Here, again, radiating curves of drapery weave the figures into unity and add decorative charm.

High on the outer wall of the cella, within the colonnade, a third type of architectural sculpture was employed: a continuous frieze. This gives an intimate and comprehensive record of the city's most solemn religious procession, that in honor of Athena at the Panathenaea. In the joyous gathering are young horsemen riding along, men in chariots, musicians playing the lyre and flute, men and women bearing gifts in jars or on trays, sacrificial animals, and the state officials, all converging toward the assembly of gods seated over the entrance to welcome them. The scheme is one of great interest and complexity. On over five hundred feet of frieze no two figures are identical; spirited action alternates with preparation and rest; the procession of worshippers proceeds, constantly but never abruptly changing, to the scene of offering over the temple entrance. Many devices were used to add to the picturesque effect. The bodies were placed in different poses, some facing in profile, others in three-quarters position; shields emerge a bit obliquely, but never so sharply as to disturb the fixed planes of the outer surface and background or check the lateral direction of movement around the building. The drapery is not purely linear; it has solidity and weight of its own, but it is kept subordinate to the figures; it radiates from the background, one mass emerging from another like a flower unfolding. There is no emphasis on naturalistic detail, yet the scenes have illustrative interest and the faces are quietly expressive. Here is decorative sculpture at its best.

Buildings erected in the last quarter of the century show the tendency to sacrifice strength and amplitude to greater decorative diversity. The temple of Hephaestus (the so-called Theseum), the Athena Nike temple, and the Erechtheum are graceful, but lack the dynamic vigor of the Parthenon. They are representative of the looser social fabric of the period. Their sculptural decoration likewise shows a lack of logical organization. The

Porch Maidens of the Erechtheum are lovely in themselves, but to use the female form as a supporting column is structurally indefensible; and the metopes of the Hephaesteum and the friezes on the Athena Nike temple and the Erechtheum are picturesque rather than impressive. The Victories on the parapet of the Nike temple are exquisite separate figures in their richly patterned drapery, but they are not woven into any organic unity and the drapery insistently calls attention to its own beauty. Individualistic variety, in keeping with the trend of the times, was sought rather than organic design.

Before we leave architecture and its accompanying sculpture, it should be noted that the buildings were planned co-operatively by architects, sculptors and state officials, with the further help, no doubt, of popular comment and criticism. Such collaboration is a sign of the artistic health of the Athenian community. A similar situation prevailed in other great creative periods of architecture, notably in Egypt and medieval Europe. A modern example is the Nebraska State Capitol, in the planning of which a leading American architect, sculptor, and philosopher combined with statesmen to produce one of the most impressive buildings of our times.

If we were to choose a single art as most representative of the Athenian democracy, it would probably be sculpture. Perhaps more than any other art it was enjoyed by the people. Objective in their thinking, they naturally liked sculpture, the art that more than any other deals with pure form. Keenly aware of physical beauty, they welcomed a permanent record of lovely human bodies. They also valued the utility of sculpture in commemorating the founding of the city, in honoring the gods and traditional heroes, in glorifying statesmen and athletic victors, in recording ancient victories in war.

Sculpture went through an evolution similar to that of painting and architecture, and at its best achieved a similar synthesis. The late sixth-century statues of maidens on the Acropolis have elaborately bordered Ionian costumes bright with color. Reliefs of athletes made about the time of the Persian invasion emphasize decorative designs of muscles and drapery, but there is increasing energy in the forms. In sculpture of this period there is an eager exploratory spirit, fresh and buoyant vitality, a lively sense of technical progress. After the Persian wars, when security and confidence had been established, there was the development of simpler and stronger motifs in both subject matter and style; moments of violent action were not represented so much as the resolution before and the reflection following action; decoration became reduced to a minimum, and the planes of the carefully observed body were amplified. Now there was developed in sculpture the same process which we have observed in the other arts: a synthesis of Doric power and Ionic grace. It appears in Myron's Discobolus, a finely co-ordinated design, in which a healthy, hardened athlete's body starts its well-poised swing; in the Artemisium Zeus; in Cresilas' portrait bust of Pericles; and in many lovely gravestones.

Toward the end of the century there came an increased emphasis on graceful incident, sensuous effects, and realistic detail. The sculpture of this period is superior to previous work in anecdotal interest and surface modulation, but its organization is far weaker.

In the sculpture of the Periclean period we see Athenian art at its best. Vigorous modeling, sensitive handling of line, the intellectual organization of compositions, the realization of emotional serenity and vigor in disciplined mass: all have never been more ably done than by Phidias and his fellows. This sculpture may properly be called idealistic. Instead of representing a face or figure with emphasis on its stripped geometric structure (abstraction), its highly individualistic traits (realism), or a momentary phase of its loveliness (impressionism), the sculptors worked out conceptions built up from many impressions and observations, eliminating the less important elements until only the essential ones remained; these they amplified, creating sculpture in capital letters.

So the Athenian sculptors met the intellectual and emotional needs of their fellow-citizens, and educated them by representing men and women as they would at their best wish to be. And to their sculptors, the few distinguished artists and the many able craftsmen, the people gladly entrusted this public service.

THE NEW EDUCATION

As Pericles pointed out in the Funeral Speech, education in Athens was regarded as far more than formal training for young people; it was actual participation in the political, social and aesthetic activity of the state which produced the independence of mind, versatility of accomplishment, and richly developed personality which he affirmed to be the possession of the citizens of Athens. But formal education was also a factor in the development of good citizens.

Here, again, certain reservations must be made. There

were no schools for girls; as Socrates said, a girl learned from her parents "the duties which would be hers in later life": the management of household affairs, cooking and weaving, the training of young children. And for the boys there was no system of education controlled by the government, with the exception of military training between the ages of eighteen and twenty. All citizens were required, however, to send their boys to elementary private schools, where they were taught reading, writing and arithmetic, music, literature and gymnastics, up to about the age of fourteen. Beyond this the children of the poorer parents had no formal instruction.

Parents who could afford to do so continued the education of their boys with more advanced physical education, music, literature and mathematics, to which was added a certain amount of history, natural science and philosophy.

Opportunities for physical training were provided for all at public expense. There were many gymnasia in Athens, where any one was free to exercise and could receive instruction. These gymnasia, like the marketplace, were also centers of discussion regarding public affairs and of more or less philosophical speculation.

About the middle of the fifth century B.C., this traditional education began to be supplemented by the instruction of a group of itinerant teachers known as Sophists. Eager to acquire new knowledge themselves by travel, and realizing the market for the sale of their intellectual wares in a place as intellectually curious as

Athens, they made that a center of their activity. When a Sophist reached the city, often as the guest of a wealthy man, groups of young men would hasten to register in his informal class, paying a good price for the privilege. Of course, only the wealthier ones were able to afford such a luxury. Their motives in seeking instruction were doubtless mixed. It was the thing to do; it made them more interesting social companions; it opened up new avenues of information and theory to the intellectually alert; and, perhaps most of all, it promised young men training in useful information, public speaking and psychology which would enable them to exercise influence in the assembly and the courts.

It is not strange, therefore, that much of the education offered by the Sophists was extremely practical in character, similar to the courses in the art of persuasion and the development of personality which are so popular today. But the more conscientious Sophists were not satisfied with giving such superficial training. They were genuinely concerned about the problems of human personality, the process of thinking, the social institutions which men had created, and the latest aesthetic and scientific theories. They introduced a spirit of speculation regarding traditional customs and beliefs which, during the last part of the fifth century, was exercising a tremendous influence on Athenian life. Their own attitude was sometimes conservative, sometimes radical, but the general effect of their teaching was to encourage a skepticism that was deeply resented by people who clung to traditional ways of thinking.

One of the greatest of the Sophists was Protagoras, a self-made man of humble origin, who believed strongly in the ability of ordinary men to control their lives by the use of common sense trained by careful methods of thought. Why speculate about the nature of the physical world? he asked. "The proper study of men is themselves and their human institutions." It is also useless to speculate about the gods; we have no sure way of knowing whether they even exist or not, and life is too short to waste it on such inquiry; all we can have are opinions, which of course may be helpful. What men can pursue to advantage is the study of themselves and the means by which they may live together on mutually useful terms. So he stated that social virtue, like any other art or craft, could be taught, and advertised that he taught it.

This theory of Protagoras was obviously based on the democratic assumption that men are capable of self-direction and social collaboration, and contrary to the aristocratic belief that only a few have the native ability to govern or to maintain a well-regulated state. His doctrine that "Man is the measure of all things" has been interpreted to mean that there is no generally valid truth or morality, that each individual knows only what is good or true for himself; but more likely he meant that by the co-operative judgment of mankind social knowledge of a practical sort is attained.

Of the other Sophists, Gorgias, Prodicus and Hippias were outstanding. Gorgias appealed especially to those who wanted training in the effective use of language for literary, political and legal purposes; in his courses he analyzed the meanings of words and the principles of forensic style. He also protested against devoting time to the study of physics, on the ground that the nature of the material world with which physics deals cannot even be proved to exist; even if it did exist, it would be unknowable to us; and even if it were knowable, the knowledge could not be communicated by one person to another. Prodicus' specialty was also the exact and effective use of language.

There was, however, a more radical group of Sophists. The most famous was Hippias, who, in addition to the unusually varied curriculum which he offered, advanced the theory that while men differ in their customs and laws they all have the same natural endowment, whatever their race or birth. Here was stated for the first time the doctrine of natural rights which was destined to play such a large part in later democratic theory; it involved, of course, a denial of the traditional Athenian relegation of women and slaves to an inferior status. This theory was further developed by later Sophists into a defense of extreme individualism. Starting from the assumption that laws and customs are merely conventions, they held that no particular government need be regarded with respect or obeyed. But if government is changing and unimportant, that is not the case with the nature of each person;

in their pursuit of pleasure all men are essentially alike. Therefore laws may be broken if they interfere with the individual's right to pleasure; all that is needed is a means of breaking them successfully.

From this developed a new theory of justice: that when two individuals or groups conflict, justice is simply the interest of the stronger. Since governments operate only in the attempt to keep powerful people from realizing the pleasures to which they have a right, thus producing a slave morality, the strong are justified in asserting their superior power. Might is the only right. We have already seen how this principle was applied in the Athenian treatment of Melos.

It is not surprising that many of the young aristocrats, feeling that the democracy had robbed their class of its proper prestige and control of the government of the city, accepted such a philosophy with eagerness. Now they could pursue their pleasures with the assurance of their right to have them, and exercise their will to power with the conviction that they deserved to rule. Many of the young democrats likewise found this theory to their liking. It seemed to them to justify the individualism for which Athens was noted among Greek cities and the imperialistic policy of domination over the so-called allies.

This growing scorn for established customs and this shameless pursuit of personal pleasure were looked upon with apprehension by many Athenians, aristocratic as well as democratic groups. The aristocrats had a nostalgic regard for the customs of an earlier Athens, which remained as the code of their class; the democrats had an equally fervent respect for contemporary democratic concepts. So the economic conflicts of the last part of the fifth century were accompanied by a bitter controversy of opinions among the people, which increased both the tension and the lack of unity.

Another teacher who became prominent at this time was Socrates. In some respects he was like the Sophists, although his instruction was most informal and he asked no pay for it; he, too, won an eager following among the young intellectuals of Athens. He was born of working middle-class parents. Early in life he became interested in the speculations of the physicists regarding the nature of the physical world, but became dissatisfied with their materialistic interpretations and turned to the study of human thinking and conduct. Unconvinced by the pragmatism of Protagoras or the materialistic individualism of the more radical Sophists, he came to the conclusion that the Sophists did not probe deeply enough: thinking was a more exacting exercise than they realized, and human relations had a more fundamental basis than they had discovered. He was also appalled by the superficial judgment of political leaders, whose opinions masqueraded as knowledge and whose actions were stupid, impulsive and selfish. Possessing a strong sense of social duty, seasoned with humor and humility, and a lively interest in people which saved him from superciliousness, he set forth on the mission of working out principles of sound thinking which would save men from what he considered to be their folly.

Why do men act foolishly and disastrously? he asked. Because they do not know any better. Once a man achieves genuine knowledge he is necessarily virtuous, for it is inconceivable that any one can know what is right and not do it. Every one wishes to do what is good (in characteristic Greek fashion Socrates identified individual and community welfare), and fails only because he is ignorant.

Such knowledge, Socrates declared, must be distinguished from specialized mastery of particular skills. A man may have expert knowledge and be technically "good" at his job, yet be grossly uninformed with regard to the principles and practice of good conduct. In fact his unquestioned ability in his own field may be a positive disadvantage in that it leads him to an unjustified confidence in his mere opinions outside that field.

How, then, is comprehensive knowledge to be attained? By applying to all of our experience the critical faculty of reason. "The uncritical life is not worth a man's living." Most men live on the basis of habit or opinion, which may result in satisfactory conduct, but neither gives any guarantee of consistency because in neither case is there real understanding. The only procedure which gives promise of certainty is the critical analysis, definition, and synthesis of the concepts which guide our activity, such as courage, equality, friendship and justice, so that we will agree on their meaning and see their relation to one another. Socrates came increasingly to believe that knowledge is thus a weaving of separate ideas into the pattern of their total relationships; any part of life is only to be understood in view of the whole; and our intellectual and moral growth is from the particulars of experience to as consistent and unified an interpretation as we are able to make.

In 399 B.C., an Athenian court condemned this man to death. Behind the specious charges was the obvious belief that he was subversive of the democracy. Was there any justification for this belief and this verdict?

It must be remembered that Athens was recovering painfully from the wounds of war, defeat, and the terror of the oligarchs; that the leader of the notorious Thirty had been Critias, a disciple of Socrates; that for years Socrates had exposed the ignorance and inefficiency of public men in Athens, to the delight of his intimate companions, the young aristocrats; that he was associated in the popular mind with the radical Sophists; that he had criticized the selection of officials by lot and asserted that public service was a dangerous career for honest men. It is not strange that the people should have regarded him as subversive and have been in no mood to tolerate longer a man who, in their eyes, was an outstanding critic and enemy of democracy. In all probability they would have preferred to send him into exile, but his refusal to show any spirit of conciliation at his trial spurred them on to vote the death penalty.

A courageous critic of Athenian democracy he certainly was—and a wiser Athens would have taken many of his criticisms to heart; self-analysis and the rigorous examination of one's beliefs in terms of consistent concepts are a wise prescription no matter who the doctor may be. There is some evidence to indicate that he became politically more conservative as he grew older. But it must be questioned whether he was at heart an enemy of democracy, regardless of his attitude toward specific shortcomings of Athenian administration. He liked and associated with plain people too much for that; his love for Athens and her ways was deep, in spite of her mistakes; he always obeyed her laws and refused to be used as a tool by the Thirty when they held unconstitutional power; he believed in freedom of speech; and there is no reason to suppose that he denied any man the capacity for straight thinking and unselfish action. His mission was to unmask ignorance, wherever it might be found, and to lead men to saner thinking. What the particular political consequences would be was, to him, far less important than the personal and social effect.

Regardless of the aims and validity of his thinking, his method, like that of the Sophists, contributed to the prevailing unrest during the last part of the fifth century. By itself the skepticism was a healthy thing, indicative of growth, and if it had had a peaceful environment in which to function, there is every reason to believe that the Athenian social order would have adjusted itself normally to the new education and been the stronger for it. But the interplay of the furious conflict of ideas and the harrowing flux of war allowed no such adjustment to be made; the minds and morale of the people of Athens became increasingly unstable; and when the war ended the city was left distraught in attitude as well as exhausted in resources.

9

POLITICS AND THE

DRAMA

The Greek tragedies give us no easy insight into the political beliefs of their writers. Their chief concern was with those qualities which, as Gilbert Murray has said, "speak to us across the footlights of the centuries"— beauty of structure and phrasing, the ethical and philosophical significance of human purposes in conflict against one another and against forces greater than they. To such general issues Aeschylus, Sophocles and Euripides devoted their genius.

Yet we could hardly expect playwrights for a fifth-century Athenian audience to have remained insensitive to the pressing immediate problems of their fellow citizens. Greek tragedy was an art deeply rooted in the soil of its own daily life, as well as that of universal human experience; the plays were chosen for presentation, produced, and judged by officials of the community; and that community, politically minded as few have ever been, was involved not only in exciting domestic policies but also in the creation, control and defense of an empire. It would be strange indeed if in the plays there were no reflection of such vital concerns. That there was such a reflection becomes clear when we examine the dramas more closely from this point of view.

In Aristophanes' comedy, the *Frogs*, the god Dionysus is pictured going to Hades to bring back a tragedian to save the befuddled city by his advice, and in the same comedy Euripides is made to say that a poet deserves praise when he develops better citizens and Aeschylus to boast that he did it. This claim Aeschylus tried to justify when he wrote the *Persians*, which glorifies the patriotic devotion of the Greeks in the battle of Salamis; but apart from that play we have none surviving that deal directly with contemporary events. Yet, in spite of the fact that the setting of the other tragedies was laid in the heroic past of the Greek people, and usually far from Athens, the situations chosen and the sentiments expressed must have stimulated the audiences to make contemporary applications, thus enforcing the emotional effect by associations with their own experience.

We find considerable evidence to indicate that the tragedies had political as well as philosophical and aesthetic meaning.

The most obvious way in which the dramatists revealed their loyalty to the city, and sought to arouse the patriotic feeling and thought of their audience, was by inserting references to Athens. Aeschylus, who proved his patriotism by fighting at Marathon, was equally ardent in his plays, often mentioning Athens as a beautiful and prosperous city, preserved in liberty by the gods and the citizens. Sophocles described the physical charm of its surroundings, and put praise of its power in the mouth even of its enemies. But it was Euripides who most unblushingly included comments about his mother country. His favorite epithet was "illustrious," but he also wrote of it as prosperous, a shining city, built by the gods, land of heroes, free, the lovely home of the Graces. In the *Medea* the women of Corinth were ironically made to sing the glory of their most bitter commercial rival. Even prisoners of war seemed to find solace in the thought of going to such an attractive place.

Of all its characteristics, none was approved more earnestly than its reception of refugees. Pericles' boast in the Funeral Speech, "We open our city to all the world," was repeatedly voiced by the poets. Two plays of Aeschylus dealt with this theme. Sophocles made Oedipus, seeking refuge from Thebes, declare that Athens alone gave hospitality and security to unfortunate aliens. The point was emphasized by Euripides. He pictured Medea finding refuge there when she fled from Corinth; the suffering Heracles was warmly welcomed by Theseus, and his children were received by a king who said, "To yield up suppliants to another country I consider as bad as being hanged." When exiles in the *Suppliant Women* confidently turned to Athens, declaring that it always protected the wretched, they, too, were gallantly welcomed.

The dramatists were unsparing in their criticism of the traditional enemies of Athens: Thebes and Sparta. It is surely no coincidence that they so often used the legends of Thebes, picturing the early woes of that city with its dictatorship and intolerance, incest, patricide, banishments and agony; or that so often its rulers were made to suspect their subjects of base motives.

Aeschylus described Thebes as the town of the god of war, whose ruler declares: "Anyone who refuses to obey my authority shall die." Sophocles showed in the *Antigone* how such tyranny results in disaster, and in the *Oedipus at Colonus* foretold how Thebes would one day be defeated by the free city of Athens. Euripides was especially bitter toward the Thebans. The most dastardly tyrant in Greek drama is Lycus, a native of that city. In the *Suppliant Women* the Thebans are condemned as "insolent and evil-hearted," and their cruelty is vividly contrasted with the warm human sympathy of Theseus of Athens.

But Euripides' most bitter criticism was directed at Sparta. Sparta is "heartless and variable in her ways"; her king, Menelaus, is insolent and brutal toward women and children, cowardly, deceitful and shameless. The *Andromache*, written during the early years of the war, rings with the most violent denunciation of the Spartans: if their military reputation were taken away they would be accounted utterly worthless; their morals are scandalous; undeserving of their good luck, they are "the most hateful of men, tricksters, lords of lies, weavers of evil, crooked, unhealthy and devious in mind, wholesale murderers, lustful for gain, always saying one thing but contriving something else." Seldom has patriotic hostility found such spirited expression on any stage!

Much of this patriotism might have served a purely nationalistic purpose, but as we examine the attitude of the three tragedians toward the evolution of democracy in Athens the political references become more significant.

Aeschylus, himself a member of the landed nobility, during the time of Cimon's conservative leadership rejoiced in the responsible freedom which Athens had achieved for her citizens; she had guaranteed personal liberty for all, and because of her victory at Salamis those cities which were previously subject to Persia had regained freedom of speech and action. "Who is master of the Athenian people?" the Queen Mother of Persia inquires, and the Chorus replies, "Of no man are they called the slaves or subjects." In the *Suppliants* he represented the acts of the good king as determined by the will of the people. But as time went on, he grew somewhat apprehensive regarding the radical tendencies of the democratic movement, especially its overthrow of the powers of the traditional court of the Areopagus. In the *Eumenides* Athena warns the citizens against anarchy as well as tyranny, and advises them to regard with reverence the ancient customs. According to Plutarch, when the audience heard Amphiaraus described, in the *Seven Against Thebes*, as a man of modesty, integrity, and profound insight, they all turned and looked toward Aristides, that conservative leader, believing that the words were meant for him. Whether or not the story is true, the implication is doubtless correct; Aeschylus admired such elder statesmen.

It is fair to conclude that Sophocles was warmly in sympathy with the middle-of-the-road democracy. His most eloquent argument for it is the *Antigone*, which must be regarded as a democratic document of the utmost importance. The conflict is between a new autocratic ruler of Thebes, Creon, and Antigone, his niece, who refuses to obey his public order to leave unburied the body of her brother, whom Creon has stigmatized as a traitor to the city. But this conflict is not merely between an individual's sense of personal love and religious duty and the governmental authority opposing it; Sophocles saw that human situations are seldom as simple as that. Antigone stands for the self-respect of her family as well as her own (Sophocles is plainly aware of the value of traditional family loyalties); she is strongly conscious of being a woman who is being given orders by a man; and in her bitter refusal to share the distinction of martyrdom with her sister she is somewhat arrogant as well as un-questionably courageous. Creon is likewise governed by a variety of motives: he is genuinely patriotic; he is very much aware of his power and apprehensive of losing it; he hates Antigone as a personal opponent, especially since she is a woman. The problem Sophocles raises, then, is this: when two such people, both proud and inflexible of will, cherishing what they believe is right, oppose each other, what alternative to tragedy is possible? The im-plied answer can only be the democratic one—reasonable discussion and adjustment of differences by mutual con-cession.

The criticism of dictatorial rule in this play is unspar-ing, and Haemon, the king's son, makes the need of con-sulting public opinion very explicit:

Creon: Am I to govern this land according to my own views or those of other people?
Haemon: The state which one man owns is no state at all.
Creon: Isn't a state supposed to belong to its ruler?
Haemon: You would be a wonderful ruler of a desert! [1]

(Compare with this Pericles' words: "Our government is controlled, not by the few, but by the many . . . All of us share in considering and deciding public policy, in the belief that action is sure to fail when it is undertaken without full discussion.") When Creon insists that a ruler must be obeyed, whether his orders be right or wrong, for the sake of public order and efficiency, Haemon again disagrees with him sharply; the resentment aroused among the people when their judgment is disregarded, he declares, undermines any real stability.

In the *Oedipus the King* and *Electra*, written after the outbreak of the Peloponnesian War, we can discern less enthusiasm for the prevailing spirit of the people. The line, "What hate and envy accompany outstanding excellence!" is doubtless a veiled comment on the current criticism of Pericles, and "Set in the midst of evil, we must do evil, too" may reflect the poet's sad awareness of the growing cruelties of imperialistic policy. The *Philoctetes*, written after twenty years of war, is an especially penetrating analysis of the tragic situation developed under the empire. Young Neoptolemos has high individual standards of honor and kindness; Odysseus, arguing that public expediency in a time of crisis cannot afford such virtues, tries to make him become dishonest and cruel. Here is a dilemma which must have seemed very real and perplexing to the Athenian audience, and it is not strange that Sophocles required a *deus ex machina* to resolve it. In the character of Odysseus we see pictured the type of politician that Sophocles plainly disliked: the man who exercises control by specious words rather than just deeds, and who feels no shame in causing suffering to innocent people if the success of his schemes depends upon it.

The conservatism of Aeschylus and the moderate liberalism of Sophocles did not satisfy Euripides, who showed throughout his plays a profound understanding of common people, including women and foreigners, and confidence in their integrity and good sense. He manifested sympathy for the followers of the popular god, Dionysus, who "has no scorn for the humble, but freely gives his wine to all"; the lowly, even slaves, he held in respect, declaring "It is the name only that brings shame on the slave," and "The honest man is nature's nobleman." We would therefore expect him to favor the more radical democratic policy, in internal affairs if not in its imperialistic objectives.

Often in his earlier plays Euripides stated the superiority of democratic rule over dictatorship. In the *Suppliant Women* Theseus declares: "I have made Athens a free city, with equal votes for all. Our city is not ruled by one man; Athens is free, the people rule it, and they bestow equal rights on rich and poor." An Argive herald and he proceeded to debate the subject. The herald argues that in a democracy the ignorant mob rules, and demagogues, previously nobodies, control the people for personal gain. Theseus replies that there is no worse foe to a community than a dictator, under whom equality before the law vanishes and the weak and poor are oppressed; but in a democracy, youth, wisdom and excellence have a fair chance to serve the common welfare. These sentiments were often repeated by Euripides. Despotic rule is declared to be injustice masquerading as prosperity; a dictator chooses vile men for his friends, and must always live in fear of death.

But the privileges of democracy also entail responsibilities. Echoes of Pericles' Funeral Speech appear in the *Children of Heracles*, when Iolaus speaks of the duty of a good man to subordinate self to the common good, and Macaria gladly gives her life for the safety of the city; also in the *Hippolytus*, where apathy and the pursuit of pleasure are deplored, and in the *Suppliant Women*, where the ideal citizen is described.

As the war dragged on, Euripides began to realize, in spite of his faith in democracy, the dangers inherent in it which were being realized under the stress of the struggle. The most spirited indictment is stated by Ion, who says that the mass of men hate those who are wiser than themselves, especially those who mind their own business in a city "full of criticism"; demagogues fear unselfish youthful ardor and real merit, and crush them. A similar charge is made by Hecuba, who warns against the rabble which makes a man act contrary to his better judgment because of the fear of popular disapproval. "Terrible are the rabble when they have bad leaders," says Orestes. Against such leaders Euripides directed his most sharply barbed shafts, for he still believed in the essential good will of the "unnumbered men"—the word recalls Lincoln's observation that God must love the common people, because he made so many of them. It is the glib of tongue who lead the people astray, the unprincipled seekers after power who will use any means to win control; these men he lashed unmercifully as the enemies of the state. It may be inferred that he had one of these radical demagogues in mind when he described "a man of unbridled speech, blustering in insolence, relying on sheer noise and boorish licence, yet credible enough to involve the citizens in mischief." "When a person of persuasive words but evil intentions wins the crowd to his will, it bodes ill for the city."

Pondering on these evils of an unbridled democracy and the civil strife which it engendered as the war continued, Euripides apparently came to the conclusion (as Aristotle did later) that in a dominant middle class lay the best hope of stability and civic welfare. He grew heartsick over the factional wrangling in Athens. It is the greed of the rich and the envy of the poor, he declared, that bring about such strife; but "the middle class saves states, guarding that order which the community establishes"; good will and moderation are the saving virtues.

In spite of their praise of Athens and their vigorous denunciation of her enemies, the playwrights were by no means eager to sing the glories of war and empire; their international predilections, it appears, were for peace and for a spirit of conciliation. Aeschylus praised men who defend their country, but war waged on foreign soil he viewed quite differently. How vivid is the picture of the soldiers' ordeals and the suffering of non-combatants given by Clytemnestra, the Chorus, and the herald in the Agamemnon! Sophocles, in the Ajax, described war as a shame and reproach to Greece, the cause of pain and sorrow, the plague and ruin of men. But both yield to Euripides, who came to detest with utter loathing the effects that war had wrought on men and cities, especially as he saw the brutality with which Athens forced to submission her so-called allies. After one of these outrages, in the *Hecuba* and *Andromache* he portrayed with deep compassion the woes of helpless captives. Later, in the *Suppliant Women*, the lament of mothers and children over their dead must have poignantly recalled their losses to the audience in the theatre; and for the young Athenians needlessly slaughtered in the Sicilian expedition he wrote a touching epitaph: "They, the glory of their fatherland, have vanished, vanished, they have left the plain where horses' hoofs thundered and the gymnasiums where youths contend." His greatest anti-war play, the *Trojan Women*, must have shamed at least some Athenians to realize that a victory like the recent one over the small neutral state of Melos was in reality an humiliating defeat.

"If only you would settle these controversies by intelligence instead of by fighting!" This is the advice that Euripides gave to all Greece. We read it in the *Suppliant Women*: "Foolish states, which have the opportunity to end evils by conference, yet choose to settle them by murder ... Unlucky men, why do you seize spears and kill one another? In peace preserve your towns. Life is short, and one should pass through it as happily as one can." And in the *Iphigenia at Aulis*, produced after the fall of the empire, Euripides suggested the possibility of a Greece devoted to common interests above the claims of separate states.

But the advice was given an unheeding world. Small wonder that Euripides, heartsick at the woes self-inflicted by his people, exclaimed: "Ill-fated Hellas! I mourn for her. She has the will to create something excellent, but will become instead the laughing-stock of worthless barbarians . . . God has made Hellas sick." And in his final play, written in his Macedonian retreat far from that tragic scene, he invoked, with hopeless longing, "Her who brings prosperity, Peace."

10

CONCEPTIONS OF FATE

AND FREEDOM

One further attitude of the dramatists, a more fundamental one, remains to be considered. It has frequently
been said that Greeek tragedy was a drama of the human will crushed by fate, in which individuals had no
real freedom of choice, but were caught in a web of inevitable circumstance. If this is true, obviously the
dramatists denied two major assumptions of democracy: the freedom of the individual and his ability to
shape his own destiny. But how true is it?

When we casually read the plays we find that the

power of fate or the gods seems to play an important rôle. Do we not see the characters struggling vainly against supernatural powers that contrive disaster? Hippolytus was the victim of jealous Aphrodite; Orestes, commanded by Apollo, slew his own mother; Heracles murdered his children when driven mad by Hera; and Oedipus, eager above all men to serve his people, yet was destined to be their plague. And it is not only the plots that indicate this supernatural control of men. In reading the plays we cannot escape the constant repetition of such words as necessity, fate, chance, destiny, and God's purpose, or of such sentiments as "There is nothing stronger than awful Necessity," "Zeus by ancient Law guides Destiny aright," "Fortune, with constant ebb and flow, casts down and raises high alike the prosperous and wretched," "Drift with the changing tides of Fortune," "When was ever a man so ill-fated?" Here, seemingly, is a *leit-motif* that runs through Greek tragedies; in hardly one of them is the sentiment missing, and in several it is repeated over and over again, the burden voiced by the leading actors and echoed by chorus and messenger, and sometimes by a god who is revealed in person at the end.

So critics have neatly labeled Greek tragedy as the drama of determinism. But no one can read Aristotle's *Poetics* without suspecting that this interpretation is a superficial one. The *Poetics* is not a fanciful theory invented by Aristotle; it is a realistic analysis of the plays which Aristotle had seen, a grammar of art based on the living speech of the Athenian theatre. We may credit him with at least as much insight into the meaning of Greek tragedy as later critics have had. Yet in the *Poetics* no mention is made of any such conflict against fate. Instead, the cause of the tragedy is attributed to a flaw in the character of the victim: his ignorance, passion or moral weakness; and the only necessity mentioned is this: that the consequences shall follow as a credible outcome of such traits of character and shall be consistently developed, through cause and effect, to form an organic whole. To see a virtuous man face unmerited misfortune, says Aristotle, is not tragic, but shocking; no good play has used such a situation, or one that relies on mere chance for its outcome. In so far as fate or the gods enter the scene, Aristotle apparently considered their part as incidental, without significance in the tragic dénouement; and the only superhuman compulsion which he implied is that of the complete universal structure in accordance with which any man must regulate his life if he is to achieve happiness.

Why, then, did the dramatists make such use of oracular commands, why do the gods seem to intervene so often? Aristotle again gives the answer: dramatists borrowed their plots from the historic legends of the great families of Greece, which were rich in tragic implications. But these stories, going back to early times, were dyed dark with an unquestioning faith in the control of human affairs by ineluctable fate or capricious gods, who played with men as they would and whose purposes one could neither understand nor justify. This is the framework on which the fifth-century writers constructed their plots; supernatural intervention belonged in the stories and was not expurgated in the new versions.

But if it was not deleted, it was at least modified in many ways. The word *aisa*, so commonly used in the *Iliad* as a decree of god or the destiny of a man, occurs rarely in Aeschylus and only four times in all the extant plays of Sophocles and Euripides. *Anagke* (necessity) often comes to mean the human necessity to surrender to superior force, public opinion, and natural desire, or to death, which is certainly the common fate of us all. *Tyche* (chance) implies in many instances nothing more than ordinary uncertainty, opportunity, or good and bad luck as we roughly use the terms. *Ate* (doom) is the consequence of *hybris* (presumptuous pride), or simply any bane or pest; Creon calls Antigone and Ismene by that name when they exasperate him. *Moira* and *to pepromenon* (what is allotted) usually mean simply death. *Daimon* (the divine power that distributes fortune to men) is as loosely used as *tyche* to refer to disaster.

It is also very important to examine under what circumstances such words were used, and by whom. They do not often affect the choosing of what one should do; they are invoked by a person who fears the consequences of a choice, or, when it has turned out badly, says in self-justification, "It had to be." All of us have such a tendency to evade our own responsibility.

Most often the Chorus, being unable to act themselves, take pleasure in lugubrious references to fate. How irrelevant their comments may be appears in one of the loveliest choral songs, sung to console Admetus after the death of his wife, Alcestis. A. E. Housman translated it as follows:

In heaven-high musings and many,
   Far seeking and deep debate,
Of strong things find I not any
   That is as the strength of Fate.
Help nor healing is told
In soothsayings uttered of old,
In the Thracian runes, the verses
   Engraven of Orpheus' pen;
No balm of virtue to save
Apollo aforetime gave,
Who stayeth with tender mercies
   The plagues of the children of men.

She hath not her habitation
   In temples that hands have wrought;
Him that bringeth oblation,
   Behold, she heedeth him naught.
Be thou not wroth with us more,
O Mistress, than heretofore;
For what God willeth soever,
   That thou bringest to be;
Thou breakest in sunder the brand
Far forged in the Iron Land;
Thine heart is cruel, and never
   Came pity anigh unto thee.

Thee too, O King, hath she taken
    And bound in her tenfold chain;
    Yet faint not, neither complain:
The dead thou wilt not awaken
    For all thy weeping again.
They perish, whom gods begot;
The night releaseth them not.
Beloved was she that died
And dear shall ever abide,
For this was the queen among women,
      Admetus, that lay by thy side.

Not as the multitude lowly
    Asleep in their sepulchres,
    Not as their grave be hers,
But like as the gods held holy,
    The worship of wayfarers.
Yea, all that travel the way
Far off shall see it and say,
Lo, erst for her lord she died,
Today she sitteth enskied;
Hail, lady, be gracious to usward;
      that alway her honour abide.[1]

In spite of these solemnly beautiful sentiments assuring Admetus that his wife was bound by a fate which no one can escape, the audience knows at the time, and the Chorus soon will know, that Heracles is cheating fate and restoring Alcestis to life.

Yet we must not paint the picture too brightly. In spite of all our reservations there is a fatalistic *motif* running through Greek plays, and it often seems that the gods, or fate, or chance, are the real "masters of the show." What freedom, we may ask, is left for men? Aeschylus, Sophocles and Euripides suggest four kinds of human choice. By understanding what they are we shall become acquainted with the essential thinking of the dramatists and their Athenian audience.

First, they say, men who admit that consequences will be determined by powers beyond them realize that they have no sure means of knowing what those consequences may be, and therefore make their decisions on the basis of what seems to them best. We cannot know what Zeus is, let alone the course his judgments will take. In the *Trojan Women* Hecuba prays to Zeus, "Whether thou be the necessity of Nature or the intelligence of mankind." Aeschylus, in the *Suppliants*, says that although Zeus' will is accomplished, still "the pathways of his understanding are beyond our searching out . . . in mysterious ways he executes his purposes." Since a man has no clear foreknowledge regarding what Chance may have in store for him, why should he care? asks Jocasta in *Oedipus the King*; let him make the most out of life while he can.

A further cause of uncertainty is the feeling that the powers above find it hard to decide what should happen. Divinities often oppose one another; Apollo disputes the claims of Death, Aphrodite and Artemis are at odds over Hippolytus. The Chorus in the *Agamemnon* believe that "one purpose ordained of the gods restrains another from winning the advantage." In the *Eumenides* Athena has to

weigh two claims of seemingly equal necessity, and admits that either decision will be unfortunate. When, in
the *Libation Bearers*, Clytemnestra argues that Fate must
share the responsibility for her having killed Agamemnon, Orestes replies curtly, "Then Fate has arranged for
your death, too," and proceeds to give reasons why he
should kill her. Since what is to be is unforeseen and so
uncertain, we can act only on our best judgment or most
urgent desire, hoping that our decision is the lucky one.

But the dramatists indicate that we are not left alto-
gether in the dark to determine our choice. Experience
has shown that the gods dislike such things as pride,
excess, the lust for power, inhospitality, treachery and
cruelty, because punishment has been visited on men
who thus offend. And in particular instances definite
warnings have been given through oracles and omens,
although it is suggested (especially by Euripides) that
the priests and seers who expound these warnings are
often unreliable interpreters, more concerned about personal profit than divine truth. But if the gods give such
advice they do not compel men to heed it. The result of
disobedience is ruin, but we are permitted to choose
whether or not to obey.

We may instance Agamemnon, who of his own free
will decided to sacrifice Iphigenia, hardening his heart in
order to avoid popular resentment and win a war, and on
his return home consented to enter his palace with Oriental ostentation, preferring heaven's displeasure to further
argument with his insistent wife. Xerxes in his presump-

tuous pride dared to insult the gods of Greece. Oedipus, after he had been warned that he would slay his father, followed his rash impulse in murdering an old man at the crossroads, and later, truculent, suspicious, and inflexibly confident of his own sufficiency, refused to respect the feelings of Tiresias and Jocasta. The arrogance of Ajax as a fighter led to his death, that of Pentheus as a lawmaker and moralist brought him low.

Furthermore, the gods aid men who, of their own steady judgment, choose to act well. "God loves to help the man who works to help himself," says Aeschylus. In *Iphigenia among the Taurians*, Pylades says, "Wise men take advantage of opportunity, not letting Fortune slip," and Orestes replies, "Fortune will, I think, be our ally. If a man strives zealously, God's strength helps him the more." Throughout Greek tragedy the sentiment is clear —men are warned what to avoid, but are free to choose as they will. Those who give way to their own weakness are at least accomplices of the gods in the resulting calamity.

There is, however, a more difficult problem of choice to face. It sometimes happens that the gods or fate is apparently opposed to the standards of right and wrong which the best intentioned and supposedly wisest of human beings cherish. Then, say the tragedians, we are not free to escape our destiny; but we are at least free, knowing the consequences, to decline the possibility of avoiding them by cowardly compromise. We can choose to save our own integrity. Prometheus recognized the superior power of Zeus and the inevitable penalty, but none the less defied the orders of a jealous and pitiless god; accepting his punishment, he refused to call it just. Why should the Trojan women suffer? They, too, must bear an undeserved fate, but Hecuba voices their moral victory over circumstance when she says, "The good man's native quality is never destroyed by misfortune, but always keeps its value." Cassandra is certainly morally superior to Apollo, her persecutor, when she casts the insignia of her prophetic office away; and the compassion of Theseus and the dying Hippolytus for each other should have made Aphrodite blush.

We have thus far found three kinds of choice open to men who, nevertheless, realize that the consequences are controlled to some extent by superhuman powers. But in many plays the sense of even this ultimate determinism grows dim and largely or totally irrelevant; characters come more and more to disregard the fact that the gods and fate exist; in choosing what course they shall follow they act on the basis of human propriety and probability. Especially in the plays of Sophocles and Euripides, men frankly follow their own judgment in deciding what to do. Who will say that the strife between Medea and Jason and between Antigone and Creon is more than a conflict of human wills? No superior power constrained Jason to abandon Medea, or Medea to execute her revenge. It was Creon's sense of duty to the state and his masculine egotism that conflicted with Antigone's stubborn devotion to her dead brother. Her attitude toward fate is clearly shown in her bitter retort to the sister who told her that it was useless to oppose a dictator: "Don't worry about me. Guide your own destiny—so as to be safe!" Alcestis freely chose to save her husband's life at the cost of her own: "I die for you when it was possible for me to live." Iphigenia, in the *Iphigenia at Aulis*, and Menoeceus, in the *Phoenician Maidens*, under no compulsion, divine or human, gave their lives in willing sacrifice for their people's good. Electra acted upon no mandate from Apollo; her own conscience bade her avenge Agamemnon. Ajax willed his own death, to avoid shame. Philoctetes is reproached for his obstinacy; "It is you, you, who choose this," say the Chorus; "this misfortune comes from no outside source nor from one stronger than you are. You were free to choose wisely." Neoptolemos adds, "What fortunes the gods give men they must bear, but men who cling to self-inflicted griefs, as you do, no one can rightly excuse or pity." And in the *Bacchae*, the most spectacular of all Greek tragedies, no god forced Pentheus to oppose Dionysus; the king's egotism and puritanic concern for his people's welfare dictated his conduct, which was independent and courageous, even if shortsighted. Commenting upon it, Tiresias shrewdly declared: "I do not speak prophecy when I say that Pentheus will fall. I am judging from his senseless actions."

Such instances might be multiplied at length. Those which have been cited are perhaps sufficient to indicate what the Athenian dramatists did. They took the old stories, in which heaven and fate played so important a rôle; they made a concession to sentiment by preserving in the pattern the threads of supernatural intervention. But their own thinking outstripped tradition. They were primarily concerned with probing into the consequences of human purposes in conflict, with tracing the catastrophes of human choice. What men desire to do, will to do, reason they are right in doing, this seemed to them more than anything else exciting and significant. Greek drama was chiefly concerned with the ways of men in shaping their own destiny, with the failures and the achievements of human freedom.

Finally, let us note that the tragic error of nearly every play is an autocratic pride of mind or emotional arrogance which makes the reconciling of differences impossible. Thus the ideal of the dramatists, like that of Pericles, would seem to be the well-rounded man of sound judgment, master of his impulses, ready to discuss, eager to come to a reasoned agreement with any honest opponent: in short, the democratic man.

I N T O L E R A N C E

One of the basic tests of any society is its treatment of foreign people and its own minorities. The test is two-fold: of its liberalism in granting freedom to those who differ from the prevailing opinions and activities of the community, and of its wisdom in encouraging such differences. For experience has shown that whereas the rigid suppression of inquiry, ideas and conduct not approved by a dominant group results in sterile uniformity, their free functioning is the surest guarantee of progress. The history of scientific discovery, artistic creation, business improvements, educational, ethical and religious advance, demonstrates that only in so far as the many have been called have the few been chosen.

With regard to the treatment of minorities Greece offers two striking examples. Sparta, choosing to devote her energies to the brutal suppression of her subordinate groups, produced no creative culture. Athens, cultivating freedom of speech and action, built up a great civilization.

The liberal policy outlined by Pericles for all the residents of Athens was, as we have seen, actually worked out to a considerable extent. The political opportunity available to citizens regardless of party, the economic freedom given the metics, the degree of social freedom granted to many slaves, the toleration of anti-democratic clubs and, for many years, of such critics as Socrates, the production under governmental auspices of plays sharply critical of official leaders and programs, all indicate that freedom was a reality in Athens even during the most trying times of war.

Yet there were also definite limitations. It will be useful before we leave the fifth-century democracy of Athens to examine in greater detail how those who were outside the dominant groups were treated. In addition to the obvious facts that aliens, women and slaves were not allowed to participate in shaping political policies; that the custom of ostracism made it possible for the people to exile political leaders and others who were not acceptable to them; and that a few intellectuals were forced to leave the city and Socrates was finally put to death, there is an interesting broader pattern of intolerance that will repay study.

Was there the prejudice of Athenian superiority? It is true that Athenian birth in itself conferred certain political and economic rights. Aliens could not win citizenship or own real property. Yet this restriction was not based on any assumption that Athenians were by nature better than aliens in intellectual capacity or devotion to public welfare; it was merely a practical device to guarantee a citizenry aware of its traditional responsibility and small enough in number to profit from extensive political experience and the financial rewards for public service. In every other respect Athens welcomed, even encouraged, aliens to come to the city and stay there, realizing how much they had to offer as craftsmen, business and professional men in enriching the common life. Furthermore, as master of her empire, although Athens was manifestly unfair to the allies in many respects, there is no indication that she claimed any natural right to rule; she justified her position on grounds of the service she rendered and her military power. To have asserted any innate superiority to other Greeks would have seemed to the Athenians an instance of *hybris* (pride) properly inviting divine punishment.

With regard to non-Hellenic races, the Athenians, like other Greeks, drew a sharp distinction between themselves and such peoples, who were called "barbarians." But the word did not imply what it does today. It meant

little more than "foreigners"; and popular judgment that
they were inferior was naïve rather than arrogant. Most
nationals today have a similar sense of their superiority,
which is innocent enough unless it becomes channeled
into an aggressive dogma of domination. To some extent
it was so channeled by Athens as well as other Greek
states, which acted toward tribes on the borders of their
world as if they were "lesser breeds without the law,"
proper prey for conquest and slavery. But this attitude
was seldom explicitly stated and never universally applied; until the time of Aristotle there was no defense of
slavery as an institution on the ground that some people
were by nature sub-men. And there are many instances
of asserting the rights and abilities of alien people. Euripides, in the *Medea*, had Jason voice the prejudice when
he told Medea how fortunate she was to have been
brought by him from her barbarous country on the Black
Sea to the civilized land of Greece; but in her reply
Medea showed how specious the argument was, coming
from an egotistical cad like Jason who was treating her
in such an uncivilized way. Again, in the *Trojan Women*,
Hecuba, and *Andromache*, the women of Troy were pictured as manifestly superior in quality of mind and feeling to their Greek conquerors. Decency, justice and fine-
ness of spirit, Euripides implied, were not the exclusive
possession of any race. And Athens, in her study of the
geography and customs of foreign lands, especially the
explorations of Herodotus in Persia, Babylonia and
Egypt, showed curiosity and interest rather than conde-

scension. She knew that she had much to learn from those older, more experienced cultures.

It cannot be denied, however, that there was sex prejudice. Here the argument against the Athenian claim to liberalism is a valid one. We have already seen how many restrictions were placed on women. Beyond question men considered themselves superior. To find the causes for this pronounced masculine prejudice we must go far back into the history of the Greek people. It was not present to any like degree in the heroic age. In the *Iliad* and the *Odyssey*, women, even Helen who caused the war, were treated with great respect and affection; a bride, wooed by many suitors, had to be won with gifts instead of providing her dowry; and there is some indication of an earlier matriarchal society. But during the succeeding period of storm and stress, when economic responsibility and the control of resources came increasingly into the hands of men, a superfluity of girls and women was resented as a burden which made life still more difficult for those who had to bring them up, get them married, and support them. During this period Hesiod voiced the current criticism of the sex, which continued unabated during the following three centuries. The cause of all woe to men, he declared, was Pandora, whose curiosity let loose the flood of evils that now beset them. He advised men to be especially careful in choosing a wife; wait until you have reached the discreet age of thirty, he said, and pick a girl who lives near by so that you will know all about her and she will not be a joke to your neighbors. Perhaps it would be better not to marry at all; at least "don't get taken in by a woman, it's your barn that she is after." The most vitriolic attack against women was made by Semonides, an Ionic poet writing about 630 B.C. The gods made women in various molds, he declared: one is like a sow, wallowing about in her unkempt house and getting fat, another like a shifty fox, another like a dog.

> She runs around, prying everywhere, all eagerness to hear and find out everything, and barks about it whether she finds anything or not. She won't stop when her husband threatens her, or even when he knocks out her teeth with a rock.

Another is like a clod, interested only in eating, and not knowing enough to come in out of the rain; another is like the sea, one day all smiles and cheer, the next in a violent storm. There is only one who is endurable: the rare woman who is like a bee; her quiet industry makes life happy and honeyed; she is the joy of her husband and raises dutiful children; she dislikes gossip and gloating over scandal with other women. Lucky is the man who gets such a wife!

Fifth-century Athens showed more restraint than this, but the cool superiority in Pericles' advice to women who had lost their husbands and kin in the war may have been to the more spirited among them quite as distasteful. We see a suggestion of their resentment in the comedies of Aristophanes; in his plays, notably the *Thesmophoria-*

zusae, he also showed with considerable psychological insight the devices they used to outwit their husbands and win their little triumphs. But in the tragedies there is more substantial evidence of a growing conviction that women deserved greater consideration than they were getting. In fact it is generally true that the most intelligent and courageous characters in the tragedies are the heroines, and the spectators were obviously meant to sympathize with them in the sufferings they were forced to bear and the revenge which they took on brutal and stupid men who opposed them. The most explicit defense of women was made by Euripides in Medea's superb speech before the women of Corinth. Medea, after having saved Jason's life and sacrificed everything to help him, was abandoned when he had the chance to make a more profitable royal marriage. She bitterly declared:

On me this totally unexpected blow has fallen and ruined my life. There will be no more happiness for me, friends, I want only to die. The man who meant everything to me, my husband, has treated me with utter cruelty. What can one do? Of all things that live upon the earth we women are the most wretched. First we must get a great lot of money together to buy a husband, and then it's a master of our flesh that we take. Not to succeed in getting one brings even greater shame. Will he be kind or cruel to us, that becomes the all-important question, for you know what a disgrace divorce is to a woman. So, entering among new ways of life and customs, a bride must be a seer—she never learned that at home—in order to get on well with this man who sleeps at her side. And if by working our hardest we bring it about that our husbands stay with us without fretting, life is enviable, but if we fail we were better dead. When a man is irritated at home he goes out and has a good time somewhere else, but a wife has no one to turn to except him. Then they say that we lead a sheltered life at home, avoiding danger, while they go out to fight, but I say that's foolish talk. I'd sooner endure three times all the pains of battle than bear one child! [1]

To her plea for pity the women reply in kind, saying that it is high time a poet were found to tell the world the woes that women have had to endure in the past; but they suggest that a better time is coming. Medea, by her victory over Jason in argument and her final tragic triumph, demonstrates that one woman at least, fighting alone against the most powerful enemies, has vindicated the rights of her sex.

The fact that such plays, in which intelligent and brave women prove their superiority to men, were popular in Athens is evidence that the power of the masculine prejudice was weakening toward the end of the fifth century.

There remains the question of minority opinions with regard to religion. In Athens, as in all of Greece, the community religion was an intimate and vital part of the personal and official life of the citizens to a degree difficult for us to realize. Their patron gods were devoutly worshipped by the farmers, business and professional men, and guilds of workers; divinities were regarded as protectors of family welfare and the interests of the state. Under such circumstances it is significant of Athenian tolerance that although acts of sacrilege, such as the desecration of holy objects and parodies of the mystery rituals, were vigorously condemned and punished, the most unorthodox beliefs of the materialistic philosophers and skeptical Sophists were given so much latitude.

That there was popular resentment against them is clear from three notorious cases. Anaxagoras was prosecuted for irreligion, probably about 450 B.C., under a new decree making nonconformity to the religious observances of the city cause for impeachment, and he had to leave Athens in order to escape death. Even though in all probability the charge was instigated by political enemies of Pericles in order to embarrass him, and an additional charge of intrigue with Persia helped to influence the verdict, the fact that such a law was passed shows that people who openly flouted the religious practices of Athens would run the risk of punishment. Again, in 415 B.C., Protagoras was indicted and had to flee from the city. Since the sale of the book in which he professed agnosticism was then forbidden and copies of it were collected and burned, it might be inferred that the persecution was on grounds of belief. But it must be noted that the action was taken during an especially critical time in the war; in his case, as in that of Anaxagoras, the people wanted to rid themselves of what they regarded as a dangerous political and social influence. This was certainly their attitude toward Socrates, against whom the charge of unbelief was manifestly specious; the real opposition to him came from indignant democrats.

It is apparent that except when political and personal animosity was also involved the law remained for the most part inoperative. The reason is doubtless that it merely required "conformity to the religious observances of the city." Many a Sophist or other intellectual of Athens who had his own ideas with regard to religion could avoid trouble without too great a strain on his conscience by participating in the community rituals. Beyond this requirement the official religion of the city was amazingly tolerant. Its very polytheism (deplored by St. Paul at a later date in his speech from the Areopagus) gave latitude which discouraged the breeding of fanatics. It was a religion primarily of ritualistic worship, which insisted on no creed or dogma, had no sacred book or united priesthood, and enforced no ethical doctrine. Consequently a wide range of individual interpretation was possible to suit the intellectual needs of its adherents. The extent to which critical, even skeptical, opinions were publicly tolerated appears in the plays of Euripides, notably the *Ion*, *Hippolytus* and *Bacchae*, in which human ethical standards were presented as clearly finer than those traditionally ascribed to certain gods.

We may conclude that in religion, as well as in other aspects of life, restraints imposed by the prejudices of the majority were few; men of varying beliefs faced life with the "fearless confidence of freedom."

12

THE EVOLUTION OF A

HERO

People express their own aims and purposes in the heroes they choose to revere. This revelation is especially telling in the case of heroes regarding whom there are few historical data, and who are, therefore, largely the imaginative creation of their admirers. In studying the way in which the Athenians felt toward Theseus, their leading national hero, we may expect to get further insight into the interests and ideals of the city; and as the prevailing conception of him changed we may sum up in his evolution that of the people who cared for him.

Prior to the rise of Athens as a political and cultural power Theseus was a figure ranking with other mythical heroes of the time preceding the Trojan War. If we may accept a much-contested line in the *Iliad*, he appears there as the son of Aegeus and the comrade of Pirithous, praised by Nestor as one of the group of "mightiest men who ever lived on the earth, who fought against the wild tribes of the mountains and completely destroyed them." The cyclic writers referred to his abduction of Helen and the consequent sacking of Athens by the Dioscuri; in the *Nostoi* mention was made of his war against the Amazons, in the course of which Queen Antiope fell in love with him; and Hesiod related his love affair with Hippe and his desertion of Ariadne because of his infatuation for Aegle. The Ariadne story was also told in the *Odyssey* and the *Cypria*, and in the *Shield of Heracles* mention was made of his war with the Lapiths against the Centaurs.

What emerges from this as to the character of Theseus? He was chiefly a fighter and a *ravisseur*, strong in battle "for rich-haired Helen's sake," or against the Centaurs and the Amazons, devoted to many women, a loyal comrade in war. In other words, he was a typical hero of the age of heroes.

By the time of Pisistratus his character had somewhat changed. He was still the warrior, to be sure; contemporary vases nearly always pictured him conquering the Minotaur. And he was still a Don Juan. On the chest of Cypselus he was represented with Ariadne, and on the Throne of Apollo at Amyclae, with Helen, a tradition in amorous adventure which Athens followed; on the François vase he heads the dance at Delos with Eriboea. But as a warrior he was gaining in grace. He became markedly Ionian in spirit, winning fame as a dancer and musician. From this period may come the legend of his being taunted as "a marriageable maiden" by stone masons at work on an Athenian temple. And he was becoming more circumspect in his love affairs. Pisistratus ordered removed from the works of Hesiod the verse referring to his passion for Aegle. Although we lack contemporary evidence it is perhaps reasonable to assume the further influence of Pisistratus in defining the personality of Theseus. The legendary connection of Theseus with Delos made him an obvious figure around which the more intimate relationship between Ionia and Athens, fostered by the tyrant, might center; and that Pisistratus also associated him with the reorganization of the Panathenaic festival is likely from the tradition that it was originally so named in the time of Theseus. In the cult of the athlete, which developed amazingly at this time, Theseus became the patron hero. Pausanias records the popular belief that "the art of wrestling was invented by Theseus, and after his time it was systematically taught." "All the Greeks," he concludes, "are accustomed to honor Theseus in the gymnasia and the wrestling schools." Undoubtedly he had been regarded as a religious and athletic hero before this time, but in the second half of the sixth century those aspects became increasingly emphasized.

The conception of Theseus as a sportsman grew in popularity during the period from 515 B.C. to the end of the Persian invasion. An examination of the vase-paintings and sculpture shows how he captured the people's imagination. On the earlier Athenian vases Heracles had been the leading hero-athlete. But from 515 to 480 B.C., there was a decided change; Theseus began to approach in popularity Heracles, the traditional hero of all Greek peoples. Instead of being chiefly the leader in the Cretan adventure he was now presented in many exploits: against the Amazons and the Centaurs and the various enemies that he overcame on his journey from Troezen to Athens. Just when the cycle of these adventures was established we cannot definitely say, but it is certain that toward the end of the sixth century he successfully challenged Heracles' superiority. The reason is clear: he was an Athenian, whereas Heracles had been adopted especially by the Dorians.

He was a hero of a different stamp from Heracles; not the mature man of might, but a youth of beauty, flexibility and grace, conquering his enemies less by force than by strategy, using intelligence, and fighting for well-defined, humane purposes. On the vases he was represented as the flower of Athenian youth, wearing delicate Ionian garments, with a wreath of ivy or flowers in his curly hair. "Amphitrite clad him in gleaming purple," wrote Bacchylides, a contemporary of these painters, "and set on his head a lovely wreath, dark with roses. He has a sword with ivory hilt slung from his bright shoulders, and two polished javelins, a Laconian cap covers his ruddy locks, he wears a purple tunic and a heavy Thessalian cape. A fiery light as of the Lemnian flame flashes from his eyes. A youth in earliest manhood, so vigorous, valiant and bold, surely a god is speeding him to bring a just doom on the unrighteous." [1]

Similarly in the sculpture of this period, at Athens and on the Athenian Treasury at Delphi, he is an athlete and warrior of a different type from Heracles. In the group in the Acropolis Museum, probably representing Theseus and Procrustes, his body is delicate and supple, totally different from the robust Heracles of the early pediments. On the Athenian Treasury the sculptors gave him a position superior to that of Heracles, and pictured him as a gracious and cultured youth.

Athena, who had previously sponsored Heracles, now often accompanied Theseus; it was she, according to Bacchylides, who sent him a favoring breeze to speed him to Crete. Whereas Heracles labored for a tyrant, Theseus fought for freedom. And at this time, if we may judge from an ode of Bacchylides and the well-known Theseus and Amphitrite painting by Euphronius, his connection with the sea was re-emphasized. Here again, Theseus typified Athenian ideals; he was not only an able athlete and an intelligent fighter, but also the son of Poseidon and master of the sea.

Just when the conception arose of Theseus as the

democratically minded founder of the Athenian commonwealth, it is impossible to say. But we may perhaps fairly assume that the notion became clearly defined following the overthrow of the tyrants.

As Athens grew to maturity, there was increased devotion to her national hero. He became even more popular after 470 B.C., when Cimon made political capital out of bringing back his bones from Scyros, burying them in the heart of the city, and formally establishing his cult. The leading Athenian painters and sculptors decorated with his exploits the chief buildings at home and abroad, including sculpture on the Parthenon, the Hephaesteum and the temple of Poseidon at Sunium, and paintings in the Theseum and the Painted Portico at Athens and the Lesche at Delphi. Phidias carved Theseus and the Amazons on the taboret under the feet of the famous statue of Zeus at Olympia; Micon in the Stoa Poikele pictured Theseus seeming to rise out of the earth to encourage the Athenian soldiers at Marathon. The vase-painters were less interested in mythological scenes than formerly, more concerned with scenes from daily life, but they continued to picture the exploits of Theseus.

The chief record for this period is that of the dramatists, who told the story of his maturity. Aeschylus wrote at least two, Sophocles three, and Euripides five plays in which Theseus played an important part. And the great festivals, the Synoecia, Oschophoria, Pyanepsia, and the revived Delian games, bear witness to the reverence shown the hero in the great days of Athens.

How did the Athenians like to think of him then? The vase-painters evidently preferred to hold to tradition, and often presented him still as the young adventurer. But this is not always the case. On two vases, at least, there is a change in mood. The Painter of the Yale Oenochoe pictured him facing Poseidon in a serious interview, mature in his bearing. On a lecythus by the Alcimachus Painter he appears wearily enduring his punishment in Hades in consequence of his too daring devotion to his friend Perithous; he greets Heracles, not as a youth a man, but as one man another.

It was Theseus in his maturity who now received the chief acclaim. If he was still a chivalrous fighter and athlete, he was not often thought of as a debonair adolescent; he had become more sober, deliberate, and reserved; he worked for more important causes and defended the weak in a more responsible way. He was less a fighter than a statesman, with a peace as well as a war policy. "A king of equal insight and power," Thucydides characterized him. "Inform me," he says to Oedipus at Colonus; "I must have full knowledge before I come to a decision." He asks the outcast king's advice, for "it is not proper for a wise man to disregard any matter, great or small." In the *Suppliant Women* he praises "that god who first gave order to our way of life, out of chaos and brutishness," and says, "Even when we are wronged, we should bear it calmly, not giving way to wrath." Only once was he pictured as losing his patience and poise. That was when he read the note left by his dead wife, accusing Hippolytus, his son, of a monstrous crime; but from even this blow he soon recovered and repented of not having waited for proof.

Against the Amazons he waged war for the freedom of Athens, but it was more than the mere existence of the city that he had at heart. It was Athens the law-abiding democracy which he served. Over and over again the dramatists presented him in this guise, a Pericles among heroes. "I shall see to it," he declares to Oedipus, "that this state is stronger than any one man. You have come to a community that observes justice and does nothing except with due sanction of law." In the *Suppliant Women* he formulates his faith in public opinion and political rights for all. A dictator, he declares, "is the worst foe of a state, but when the people are in control the city rejoices in young citizens eager to defend her."

He was represented not only as the political champion of the ordinary citizen but also as the sympathetic friend of the weak, the suffering, and the helpless. Treating the aged Oedipus with tender consideration, he says: "I, too, was raised in exile and in foreign lands and wrestled with many perils. Therefore no stranger in trouble shall seek help from me in vain." When Heracles, in anguish over having murdered his own children in a fit of madness, does not dare to raise his head, Theseus reproaches him gently: "Why wave me back, as if you might pollute me? It was sympathy for you that brought me here. I am a friend in foul as well as fair weather." He insists upon assuming Heracles' full burden of guilt, and brings him to Athens to share his own substance. No wonder that Heracles exclaims, "An unfortunate man becomes lucky when he gains a friend like this!"

When the suppliant Argive women ask for the bodies of their dead, killed at Thebes, he does not need the suggestion given by his mother: "It is right bravely to defend the oppressed, that is what gives you your reputation." He performs the service of love, himself washing the wounds of the dead, for, he says, no one should be repelled by suffering. Then he orders the bodies to be burned before the mothers should view the wounds, asking simply, "Why increase their grief?" And the full measure of his compassion is recorded in his laments, first over his wife, then over the dying Hippolytus. It is significant that the Theseum became the refuge for maltreated slaves, and that at Theseus' festival there was a general distribution of provisions to the poor. "His tomb," according to Plutarch, "is a place of refuge for slaves and all poor people who fear those who have more power, since Theseus was their champion and helper during his life, and in kindness heeded the prayers of the needy."

Even in the latter part of the fifth century, when moral standards had declined under the influence of war, Theseus continued to be represented as irreproachable in honor and profoundly pious, untainted by the skepticism and sophistry of the times. His ability in debate showed that he was an intellectual as well as a moral leader, but his chief qualities were those of character. "I shall not deceive you. My word is my oath," he declares to Oedipus, who finds no cause to doubt him. In the same play he constantly warns Oedipus not to fail in due reverence to the gods. Even Euripides represented him as a truly religious man. He reproaches refugees for not seeking divine blessing, and condemns Adrastus for ruining his state by scorning the gods; as for himself, he says, he craves to have the good will of all the gods who reverence justice; and he prays: "Lady Athena, I shall obey your commands, for you guide me so that I may not err." It is only in the *Hippolytus* that he says, in his agony, "The gods blinded my mind."

The Theseus of the late fifth century was a man truly heroic, cast in a mold more ethical than the gods themselves, demanding respect and reverence and love, a moving figure indeed in those feverish days. We may imagine that in thinking of him the Athenians found confidence and security. The words inscribed on Hadrian's Arch: "Athens, formerly the city of Theseus," have profound meaning. Athens, while she had been the city of Solon and of Pisistratus, of Pericles and Cleon, had consistently been the city of Theseus. The reason is that he was a hero not limited by the known facts of an actual life; he had grown as the city grew, re-created after Athens' own heart, in her own best image. Paraphrasing Chesterton, we may say that she did not love him because he was Theseus; he was Theseus because she loved him.

PART THREE

The Criticism
and Decline
of Democracy

13

CONSERVATIVE

REACTIONS

So far we have been seeing Athenian democracy chiefly from the point of view of those who believed in it. But there was, of course, another side. Even before the Peloponnesian War, which brought the mistakes of popular government into high and sometimes hideous relief, there was bitter criticism among the aristocratic cliques. During the war and following its tragic conclusion, when the creative spirit of the city was at a low ebb, adverse judgments broke forth in full flood. Now, facing the decline of democracy in Greece, we must take into account the opinions of those who never believed in it, or whose tentative faith could not survive its faults.

The chief criticism came, of course, from uncompromising aristocrats. During the last half of the fifth century Athens was not a happy place for them. They had to submit to seeing common artisans and farmers deciding public policy and judging them in the courts; they resented the prevailing spirit of mercantilism and industry; their claims of ancestry and a gentlemanly way of life were ignored or ridiculed; intellectual skepticism was questioning many of their most cherished beliefs and customs; and, to crown it all, war was being waged against Sparta, a city which many of them admired and which most of them thought should be appeased.

They were favorably disposed toward Sparta because that city had what Athens lacked: a strict code of tradition, law and order firmly established, the banning of innovation. Since so many of the critics of democracy in this and the succeeding century looked toward Sparta with approving eyes, we shall do well to study its pattern of government and education.

Sparta was founded on the supremacy of a small group of Dorian invaders over the inhabitants whom they conquered, a supremacy which was never relinquished. Descendants of some of the conquered people as well as imported workers, called perioeci (dwellers-around), were assigned to the handicrafts and trade, to provide equipment for their superiors; others, the helots, did the farming to produce the necessary food. Both groups were kept in a status of absolute subordination. The perioeci received enough privileges to keep them satisfied, but among the helots revolt was always a danger, which the Spartans met by periodic murder of those who showed any unusual initiative or ambition. Thus security from the threat of the majority of its own population, which was ten times greater than the number of Spartans, was the chief problem of the state, and it was solved by the most brutal means.

Owing to this almost exclusive preoccupation, the Spartans, after attempting for a time to develop a cultural environment by importing poets, sculptors and craftsmen from other cities, by the fifth century resigned themselves to an austere life based entirely on a semi-communistic military pattern, thus reverting to a society little more advanced than a primitive tribal order. Every man until late in life was a soldier under the severest discipline, eating at a common mess and owning virtually no private property. Since the suspicion which they had toward their subject population extended also to their own ranks, they framed a government with a careful system of checks and balances. There were two hereditary kings who shared the command of the army, although they were not in complete control of military policy; a council of twenty-eight men over sixty years of age had advisory and legal duties; and the assembly of citizen-soldiers over thirty years of age met for formal discussion of city issues. The chief administrative officials were five ephors who were elected annually from all the citizens.

As a result of this elaborate distribution of powers Spartan foreign policy was usually somewhat hesitant and decidedly conservative.

In their education the Spartans showed their complete devotion to the military ideal. Up to the age of seven, boys were taken by their fathers to meetings of military clubs, to habituate them to the customs of soldiers; then, organized into divisions under drill-masters, they started their rigorous military life. The aim was to develop courage and endurance. Individual initiative was encouraged only in lying and stealing, and even those practices were drilled into groups as a part of the Spartan curriculum. The result was strong, silent, dangerous men. The educational values which Athens prized—reading, debate, the arts—were scorned in Sparta. Girls were trained to become the wives and mothers of soldiers by a similar physical regimen in organized "packs."

The result of all this was a well-regulated state from the military point of view, but sterile in every cultural way. The highest virtue was to fight and die bravely for one's country; that is what men praise and women love, declared Tyrtaeus, a poet who wrote the marching songs for the sons of military men. The simple code is summed up in one of his marches; the drum-beat rhythm of the original is roughly approximated in this translation:

> Up and on, sons of noble Sparta!
> Valiant children of citizen fathers!
> Your shields swung out on your left side,

Letting drive your spears without flinching.
Never a thought of saving your lives:
That is not done in our Sparta!

It was the law and order of this commonwealth, the discipline, the devotion to an aristocratic code of conduct, the scorn of manual labor, the suppression of the workers, that appealed to the aristocrats of Athens. Their own ideal was, of course, a broader cultural one, but they saw many administrative advantages in the Spartan system.

Of the poets of fifth-century Greece, the favorite of the aristocrats was Pindar, a Theban of noble Dorian ancestry who wrote odes in honor of the victors at the great athletic festivals. Although he showed little interest in politics (his profession perhaps made him cautious), he loved to visit the princes of Sicily who entertained with sumptuous hospitality, patronized the arts, and kept fine racing stables. All of his writings praised the traditions of gentlemen. "Wealth adorned with virtue is the true light of men," he wrote; respect for one's ancestors and their way of life is a noble thing; since the hot-headed rabble revolts against custom, leadership should be in the hands of the few who are wise and just; a devotion to honor marks the narrow road to the Elysian fields.

The philosophy which appealed most to the best families in Athens was that of the Pythagorean brotherhoods, whose chief intellectual concern was mathematics but whose practical interest lay in a determined defense of aristocratic regimes against the inroads of democracy. They approved especially of the Pythagorean loyalty to ancient laws and customs even if they might be in certain respects inferior to new ones, on the principle that change is in itself a dangerous thing, the greatest sin is anarchy, and in the nature of things some are fitted to rule, others to obey.

The opposition of the aristocrats was not, however, confined to theoretical objections. It also took the form of clubs with a program of action, which worked constantly for the overthrow of the democratic government of Athens. Their efforts were successful, as we have seen, only for brief periods in the later years of the war and after its conclusion, but their activity in stirring up resentment was unceasing. A document characteristic of their propaganda is an anonymous publication, written probably about 420 B.C., entitled *The Constitution of Athens*. This cynical little essay attempts to explain why a government of the Athenian sort could maintain itself in power or even be tolerated by decent people. It has produced a society, says the Old Oligarch, in which even slaves are given freedom and equality; where insignificant men strut about as officials, insolently enjoying the trappings of office and making private fortunes out of the public revenues; where politicians bribe the people by programs of public works and festivals, free gymnasia, and pay for judicial and military service; where treaties and alliances are repudiated by an assembly which is totally irresponsible. Toward their subject states they are unjust and rapacious. No one is pleased with such disorder except the rabble; but it is precisely the rabble who rule, so there need be no wonder that Athens keeps such an absurd system. This crusty and unregenerate Old Oligarch viewed the democracy through the jaundiced eyes of party spite; his criticism reveals how incapable his group was of understanding the social and educational value of the democratic policy.

A slightly later critic of the principles and administration of the Athenian system was Xenophon, a country gentleman of limited intellect but of lively interests, a soldier of fortune, a modest student of systems of government and education, an admirer of Socrates, a self-reliant, practical man. He wrote a book on education in Persia, approving it because it concentrated on military skill and truth-telling; the social structure of Persia he also praised for its class system, and the government for its wise monarchy. In his treatise on the management of an estate he declared that there are only two occupations fit for gentlemen: warfare and farming; "the so-called menial occupations are properly despised, for they kill the bodies of those who are engaged in them by forcing such people to stay seated indoors"; the rights of citizenship should not be extended to such deformed people. Socrates' condemnation of the selection of officials by lot and ill-considered judgments made by the assembly convinced him that this philosopher, at least, was a sensible man like himself.

But the chief spokesman for the aristocratic program was the leading comic poet of Athens, Aristophanes. Not that he was a political partisan; he had too much independence of mind to ally himself with the reactionary clubs, and he loved Athens more than any party. But he did hold up to ridicule the shortcomings of the democracy, and his background as a country gentleman made him sympathetic toward the general attitude of his class. The most convincing proof that freedom of speech was soundly guaranteed in Athens is the fact that his plays, unreservedly critical of approved policies and procedures and of majority leaders, were performed regularly during the course of the war under governmental auspices, and received many first prizes. Only once was he held up by censorship, and then it was quickly revoked.

One reason for this remarkable tolerance was, of course, that the people wanted to see the plays produced because they were full of riotous and frequently outrageous fun. They are so even to us—and humor must be good not to suffer greatly in being transplanted down the centuries. He used every trick of the comedian: puns and outlandish speech, incongruous situations, ludicrous entanglements succeeding one another at a breath-taking pace, the burlesquing of scenes from serious plays, audacious vulgarity, fantastic characters and costumes.

But, as he himself said, even a comic writer can tell the people the unpalatable truth. He was more than a comedian; he was a social and political satirist, calling attention to what he considered the mistakes which the Athenian people were making in their politics, their education, their relations with neighboring states.

In his earliest extant play, the *Acharnians*, written after half a dozen years of war, Aristophanes presented the thesis dear to the country gentlemen, that the war should never have been started and that negotiations should be entered into with Sparta to stop it. In the play we see, in addition to Aristophanes' hatred of war itself, his loathing of the crop of specious diplomats, politicians (especially Cleon, the majority leader), informers, and profiteers which had grown up like weeds in the environment of war.

Dicaeopolis (Honest-citizen) is pictured as a sensible farmer who tries to get the government to make peace with Sparta; when his efforts fail he makes a private peace of his own. This is resented by a group of Acharnians, humble charcoal burners from the hill country, who are herded inside the city and have to watch their property being destroyed by the enemy; instead of blaming their leaders, however, they are ardent patriots and want to stone Dicaeopolis as a traitor. They are finally persuaded to listen while he presents his case:

A. Here's the fellow who made the treaty, here he is, the very man. Everybody hit the rascal, hit him, hit him again!

D. Why should you do that, most revered Acharnians?

A. You ask why, you shameless traitor? You betrayer of your country, you who made a private treaty and then dare to look us in the face!

D.   But you don't know why I made it. Just listen to me.

A.   Listen to you? Never! You're going to die and be buried under the pile of stones we kill you with.

D.   My good men, leave the Spartans out of it for a moment, and listen to the terms of my treaty and see if they aren't good ones.

A.   How could they be? Sparta doesn't respect any promises she makes.

D.   I know the Spartans too, and in spite of our anger toward them we must admit that they aren't entirely to blame for the present state of affairs.

A.   Not entirely? Not entirely? You dare to say such things to us and expect us to spare you?

D.   Not entirely, I say, not entirely, and I could prove, if you gave me a chance, that they have been wronged by us.

A.   This is a terrible and heart-perplexing thing, for you to plead for our enemies.

D.   I hate the Spartans bitterly, and I'd like to see Poseidon destroy all their houses in an earthquake, for they have cut down my vines as well as yours. Yet, since we are all friends here, let's ask ourselves why we blame the Spartans for our troubles. Our own leaders—not the people of Athens, they're not to blame—but rascally fellows among us, counterfeit statesmen, worthless, spurious, kept on denouncing Megarian goods and placed an embargo on them. Now this was trifling, and the way we regularly conduct our foreign affairs. But then some of our young bloods went to Megara and stole a prostitute; the Megarians were aroused by that and retaliated by taking off two of Aspasia's light women; and it was because of these three bawds that war broke out all over Greece. For in wrath our Olympian Pericles then proceeded to thunder and hurl his lightning and stir up Hellas, enacting laws against the Megarians that read like drinking songs. Then, when the Megarians were being reduced to starvation by the embargo, they begged the Spartans to get the law revoked, and the Spartans kept asking us to do it, but we wouldn't yield an inch. Then came the clash of shields and the war was on. Some of you will say they shouldn't have done it. But tell me this, what should they have done? You know well that if you had a provocation much less than that you would go to war about it.[1]

Some of the Acharnians are convinced. Then a general, Lamachus, enters; he is represented as a blustering, stupid soldier, chiefly interested in drawing his pay as a general. A local informer is traded to a Boeotian fish dealer in pay for some eels; when the fish dealer protests that the man is too small, Dicaeopolis replies, "Yes, but every bit of him is—rotten!" Finally Lamachus returns wounded from battle, to find Dicaeopolis matching every one of his miseries with a joy of peace in the lovely countryside, with plenty of good health, comfortable shelter, fine food, dancing and merriment.

In this play the new education is blamed for making young people flippant debaters, neglecting equally their duties and their manners, and Cleon is treated with the utmost contempt as cowardly, avaricious, and vile in his personal habits.

The following year, in the *Knights*, Aristophanes continued his vitriolic attack on Cleon. The Sovereign People is represented by Demos, a dull-witted, quick-tempered, fickle old man, who is having the wool pulled over his eyes by his chief servant, who holds his position by flattering and giving presents to his master while behind his back he is cheating him and blackmailing and robbing the other servants. Two generals, Demosthenes and Nicias, realize that the only way to get rid of Cleon is to put up a rival who will be even more effective in using the same tricks on old man Demos, so they select a sausage-seller who is bawling his wares in the marketplace. He protests to Demosthenes that he is not good enough for the job.

S. S.   Tell me this, how can I, just a sausage-seller, be a big man like that?

D.   It's the easiest thing in the world. You've got all the qualifications: low birth, marketplace training, impudence.

S. S.   I don't think I deserve it.

D.   Not deserve it? It looks to me as if you've got too good a conscience. Was your father a gentleman?

S. S. By the gods, no! My folks were blackguards.

D. Lucky man! What a good start you've got for public life!

S. S. But I don't know a thing except how to read, and hardly that.

D. The only trouble is that you know anything. To be a leader of the people isn't for learned men or honest men, but for the ignorant and vile. Don't miss this wonderful opportunity! [2]

Cleon comes blustering in, and he and the sausage-seller engage in a furious battle of insults; Cleon dares his opponent to better his record in stealing and lying. The rival finally wins the favor of Demos by offering him especially tempting gifts and making him unusually comfortable; then he proceeds to open the old man's eyes, so that Demos sees how silly he has been in submitting to the flattery and robbery of his former servant. He vows that he will be on the alert in the future.

It is astonishing that such criticism of a leading statesman was permitted on the public stage, especially in war time, the more so since the charges were clearly libelous. If Cleon had been guilty of the crimes of which Aristophanes accused him he would certainly have been indicted before a court. The facts are that Cleon was the leader of the business and working-class majority, whose policies Aristophanes disliked, was prosecuting a war of which the comedian disapproved, and was forcing the rich to meet the heavy costs of the war. This was cause enough to make Aristophanes direct against Cleon his heaviest fire of invective. Although the people accepted the leadership of Cleon, they none the less liked to have a chance to laugh at him, which is good evidence that they had the versatility of mind that Pericles praised in them.

The poet must have been a happy man in 421 B.C. Cleon was dead, and peace to last for fifty years was concluded between Athens and Sparta (unfortunately Sparta failed to get the approval of her allies, and hostilities soon broke out again). Only a month before the terms were signed, Aristophanes produced his play entitled the *Peace*; it is not much of a play, but because of its subject it doubtless made a hit. It pictures a group of Athenian farmers digging up Peace, who has been imprisoned in a dungeon, singing in her praise as they work and condemning those who like fighting, whether for the fun of it, because of military ambition, or to make war profits. In this play Aristophanes again charged Pericles with having started the war and Cleon with having insisted on continuing it, and prayed for the unity of all Hellas in bonds of friendship.

His most pointed anti-war play was the *Lysistrata*, written shortly after the disastrous Sicilian expedition. In this play the women of Athens, disgusted with their husbands for prolonging the war, unite with the women of the enemy cities in using the characteristically feminine tactics of refusing to have sexual relations with their husbands until they conclude a peace. The women's comments on the mistakes of Athenian policy are often devastating. There was no need of the war in the first place; it has been conducted badly; women have suffered from it most, the mothers whose sons have died, the unmarried ones whose chances of getting a husband have vanished. The women's policy (and here we see Aristophanes' formula for a lasting peace) is to reconcile the differences between Athens and Sparta, enfranchise the resident aliens in the city, and treat the allies in a friendly way.

Two comedies ridicule the Athenian passion for making laws and serving on juries. In the *Birds*, citizens who are weary of the politics and lawsuits of Athens ("Our Athenians chirp like cicadas over their lawsuits all life long") fly up and found a new city among the birds in Cloud Cuckoo Land, but find that even there statute merchants will not leave them alone. The *Wasps* is devoted entirely to the theme of legal service. An old farmer is madly devoted to his jury duty, which gives him a chance to meddle in the private affairs of his neighbors, feel his power over them, and enjoy public pay for the privilege. He is not pictured as a vicious person, but rather as a mentally diseased one who needs medical treatment.

The new education was attacked by Aristophanes in the *Clouds*. A pseudo-Socrates, physicist and unscrupulous sophist, is pictured conducting a Little Think-Shop, in which experimental devices such as aptitude tests and the project method are used. Here Strepsiades, a farmer whose son has loaded him down with racing debts,

comes to learn how to evade payment, but he cannot satisfy the requirements in verbal gymnastics. He prevails
upon his son to attend the school. The boy, instructed
by the Unjust Reasoning in methods of making the
worse cause appear the better one, finds out not only
how to evade the debts but also how to justify beating his
father and mother, whereupon Strepsiades takes revenge
on Socrates. In the play Socrates rejects the traditional
gods and substitutes for them Cosmic Whirl, and his
Unjust Reasoning ridicules the old-fashioned training
which made boys healthy, modest and patriotic, and
boasts that it makes them dissolute, disputatious, and
successful in getting what they want, no matter how im-
moral they may be. The *Frogs* and the *Thesmophoriazusae* leveled the same sort of criticism against Euripides;
he was condemned for making his leading characters
neurasthenic products of the new morality who try to
justify their unsocial conduct by sophistic reasoning.

Finally, in the *Ecclesiazusae*, Aristophanes represented
women seizing political power which was denied them
in Athens. They get control of the government, and pro-
pose to set up a system of socialism, with community of
property and the abolition of marriage. The fact that
Aristophanes used this material for comic purposes may
indicate that there was talk of liberation for women in
Athens, and perhaps he had some sympathy with the
idea. Praxagora, the leading lady, argues that women
should rule, because

You won't find them trying out newfangled ideas all the time. And wouldn't it have been the salvation of Athens if she had let well enough alone and not always been in a hurry to change things? Women roast their barley sitting down, in the good old-fashioned way. They carry burdens on their heads, in the good old-fashioned way. . . . They deceive their husbands, in the good old-fashioned way. They love their wine strong, in the good old-fashioned way.[3]

This is fooling, but as usual Aristophanes meant something of what he said. Women are sensibly conservative; and even when they twist the good old-fashioned way to suit their pleasure they are clever about it; "no one will cheat them, for they know all the tricks." Finally, and this argument must have sounded really convincing to some of the audience, they could not make more of a mess of things than the men had done.

How effective Aristophanes' attacks were we have no means of knowing, except that Cleon tried to silence him and Socrates considered the *Clouds* responsible for creating a hostile public opinion. In many respects they were doubtless most unfair to individuals, such as Cleon and Socrates, and to public policy. They were certainly shortsighted: Athens could not return to an agricultural economy, abandoning the commercial and industrial activity which had led to the dominance of the lower middle class in domestic affairs and the empire in foreign relations; there was little promise of a constructive *modus vivendi* with Sparta. But they were of value and deserved a greater influence than they had in pointing out the dangers of demagogues at home, rash expansion abroad, and, especially, of the war which was gradually wrecking all Greece. If Aristophanes had taken a stand that was more appreciative of the genuine achievements of the democracy, if he had concentrated on the primary need of Athens to win allies rather than rule subject states, his criticism would doubtless have been more acceptable and his contribution would have been far more valuable.

How valid was all this criticism by Athenian conservatives? Part of it may be dismissed as sheer prejudice on the part of aristocrats who resented their loss of political power and social prestige. Such were their claims that ordinary people were incapable of governing themselves, that manual labor was degrading, that old traditions should not be changed. They were too biased to admit that ordinary people in Athens had shown extraordinary ability in selecting their leaders, directing domestic affairs, and managing complex relations with their empire; that manual labor had a large share in creating the cultural greatness of the city; and that the changes in education and customs represented healthy growing pains. If the order and stability dear to the aristocrats were lacking, can any society in the process of rapid evolution be reasonably expected to develop with consistent regularity and maintain the equilibrium found in a caste system?

Many of the criticisms of the more liberal conservatives, however, had greater justification, as we have already seen. Perhaps Athens needed more of a check on the immediate expression of mass judgment; the people were sometimes inclined to follow irresponsible leadership; too free a rein was given to war-mongers, malicious informers and profiteers; the policy of expansion was pursued recklessly; and unquestionably the democracy had shown indecision and hysteria at home, and cruelty toward its subject states, as the war continued. But, granting the validity of all these criticisms, the balance sheet, in view of the actual accomplishment of fifth-century Athens, was overwhelmingly in democracy's favor.

THE FADING TRADITION

There is no need of following in detail the political events of the period between the fall of the Athenian Empire and the conquest of Greece by Macedon: the unimaginative domination by Sparta, the equally sterile leadership of Thebes, the shifting pattern of alliances whereby the separate Greek cities sought to gain security and advantage for themselves. Throughout this period their autonomy was constantly threatened by the intrigues of Persia, which finally succeeded in incorporating in her empire the Greek cities of Asia Minor, and it eventually collapsed before the combined military power and political shrewdness of Philip of Macedon. The reason is plain to see: Sparta and Thebes had military strength but lacked the statesmanship to manage the states they subdued; Athens was content for the most part to play a modestly neutral rôle after her unsuccessful venture of the previous century; and Greece as a whole, lacking both leadership and the desire for co-operation, spent its resources in plotting and fighting within itself instead of attempting to reach an understanding that might have led to effective unity.

While their foreign policy was thus fumbling, within the separate states there was increasing class conflict, individualism, and a spirit of criticism which replaced the earlier creative effort. Economically the cities were not badly off, in spite of a growth in population which reduced the standard of living for many people even below what they had been accustomed to; scientific improvements were bringing about an increase in agricultural production, trade flourished, and the banking business was never so prosperous. But as private fortunes increased, social responsibility declined. In politics, although the old institutions survived, the former zest on the part of the people was gone; social discipline and a concern for the common welfare were dissipated, because of the ambition of individuals and groups for money and power and the lack of civic interest on the part of the people; professional politicians were more eager to secure personal success than to formulate sound public policy. The keynote was no longer a wholesome relationship between the individual and the community, but rather an almost exclusive concern with individual wealth and prestige.

In literature and the arts the same spirit prevailed. The new comedy dealt with problems arising out of personal and family difficulties; robust attacks on civic institutions and party leaders like those of Aristophanes were now discouraged. Tragedy likewise abandoned the major social themes of the previous century. Critical literature, especially rhetoric and philosophy, took the place of more creative expression. There were no great community building programs; instead, wealthy men patronized the architects, sculptors and painters of the time and gave them commissions for portraits and family monuments. In consequence their art lacked the substantial idealism of their predecessors' work. The three greatest sculptors of the fourth century B.C., Praxiteles, Scopas and Lysippus, developed trends which continued throughout the later history of classical sculpture; Praxiteles made sensuous representations of individuals, concentrating on attitudes of evanescent and momentary charm; Scopas realized with dramatic energy the violent emotions of fear and agony; Lysippus modeled coldly realistic statues which translated into bronze the actual form and features of local celebrities.

During this time Athens retained her democratic institutions and continued to be a cultural center for the Mediterranean world. As a consequence of the modera-

tion shown by the restored democracy toward its political opponents, no serious oligarchical movement was
active. Sporadically the city attempted to bring various
Greek states together into a coalition, first against Sparta,
then Thebes, Persia, and finally Macedon, but there was
little heart in the effort; the people were weary of war,
and wanted above all else to go about their private concerns in peace. In 378 B.C., Athens formed a new league
including parts of her former empire, with a more democratic constitution (all the other cities were represented
by a council which had equal legislative rights with
Athens), the aim being, as an extant inscription states,
"to compel the Spartans to permit the Greeks to enjoy
peace in freedom"; but this league was broken up when
Thebes supplanted Sparta. Athens occasionally considered making campaigns reminiscent of her former aggressive days, but abandoned the projects as too ambitious.
Ultimately, however, she faced the menace of Philip of
Macedon, and then had to come to a decision whether
to appease the autocrat or attempt resistance.

Two parties developed in Athens: one for conciliation
with Philip, the other for building up alliances for resistance. The latter was led by the orator Demosthenes,
whose chief policy throughout his public life was one of
opposition to Philip, as a tyrant who would reduce the
Greek cities to a condition of slavery. Believing that
Athens still had a rôle of leadership to play, as she had
in former days, he pleaded for an increase in the Athenian navy, the cost to be met by a graduated property

tax on all the residents and diversion of festival funds, a system of alliances which would put the Greek cities on a comparable military footing with Macedon, and, above all, for a rebirth of the old Athenian spirit of freedom, courage, and devotion to civic duty.

Opposed to him at the start was a considerable number of people who refused to believe that Philip really had designs on Greece, and who considered it bad policy to send aid to cities that were being attacked, for fear that Philip would consider it a cause for making war on Athens. Demosthenes replied that Philip was actually already at war with Athens, and that Athens was doomed if she remained inactive while Philip by intrigue and bribery throughout the Greek cities caused internal dissension and softened them up one by one, meanwhile declaring that he had no designs against them; that Athens could not afford to refuse to send help in the hope that neutrality would save her, for "the fact is that whatever happens to those other states is just as much happening to Athens"; and that there could be no honorable understanding with Philip.

> If any man supposes this to be a peace, which enables Philip to conquer every one else and ultimately attack you, he is mad. If we wait for him actually to declare war on us we are naïve indeed, for he would not do that even though he marched right into Attica, if we judge from what he has done to others.[1]

But the chief group who opposed Demosthenes were those who favored submission to Philip once they saw him on the march. They were a varied lot, including some Athenians who desired peace at all costs, business men who thought their private fortunes would prosper as well or better under the Macedonian, a few who were bribed to do "fifth column" work in the city, and a group of patriots who were convinced that the day of independent small city-states was inevitably past, and that it was the part of wisdom to come to as advantageous terms as possible with a ruler who had the military strength and political sagacity to unite all Greece into an effective force against the danger which they always feared from Persia.

The leaders of this party were Eubulus, an able if cautious financier, the educator Isocrates, and the orator Aeschines. Isocrates was a conservative professor, head for fifty years of the leading liberal college in Athens, and a tireless pamphleteer. In politics he was an opponent of democracy, which seemed to his tidy mind to be most disorderly; he was distressed by the class feeling, and deplored the fact that the poor liked nothing better than to tax the rich without mercy and that the rich would rather throw their money into the sea than relieve the misery of the poor. The solution he proposed was a return to the system of Solon's time, limiting the powers of the assembly, abolishing the lot, and electing to office men of property and education.

With regard to foreign policy, Isocrates had previously

warned against imperialistic adventures on the principle that Athens must become reconciled to giving up the idea of a naval empire, since that had brought about her downfall; but he hoped that Athens and Sparta could effect an alliance to oppose Persia. Most of all, however, he had wanted peace among the Hellenic states. Horrified by the constant wars and the destruction of property and the human misery that had resulted from them, he had pleaded for a Golden Rule among the Greek cities: "Treat weaker states as you would wish stronger states to treat you." But his exhortation had been without effect. Now at last he saw a solution of the problem. In an open letter to Philip he publicly announced that in his opinion there was no future for the Greek cities if they continued to be divided and in conflict with one another; it was time for them to unite under the leadership of a ruler who had the intelligence, resources, and military genius to weld them into a really powerful alliance capable of maintaining peace among themselves and of conducting a crusade against the "barbarian" Persia. His motives were excellent; but he failed to realize that any peace guaranteed by Philip would be on Philip's terms.

In reply to Isocrates' argument, which was advanced also by Aeschines, Demosthenes leveled his most violent attacks. He declared that the menace of Persia was distant and only potential, but that of Macedon was immediate and actual. He realized the advantages that Philip had: efficiency in action because the entire control of the Macedonian state and army was concentrated in his hands, great wealth to use in bribing people in the cities he coveted, shrewdness in his policy of "divide and conquer." He also recognized the shortcomings of Athens: it stupidly refused to help states nearer Macedon that might have been bolstered up as a barrier; when it finally reached a decision it failed to center responsibility squarely or to implement its legislation with practical means for action ("A decree is worthless unless you are ready to do what you vote"); the help which it sent was always too little and too late to be effective. And it was not the policies of the city that Demosthenes chiefly criticized, it was the attitude of the citizens. The glory of your past has departed, he told the Athenians; in former times citizens were less interested in making private fortunes than in enriching the city, but now they build private homes more sumptuous than public buildings; then no such hostility as now exists between rich and poor was permitted to develop; then the people controlled their statesmen, now they let them do as they please so long as they give the people doles and amusements; free speech is allowed, even to slaves, but citizens wish to hear only what is pleasant, not what might be painful but profitable; public officials who take bribes are no longer punished, and citizens in the pay of the enemy are allowed to stir up dissension, propaganda for peace, and defeatism which undermine the morale of the city.

Yet he was convinced that the Athenian principles of government and the Athenian character were vastly supe-

rior to those of Philip. Philip, he declared, was no statesman with a constructive program; his policy had always
been one of terrorism; his success was achieved merely by
employing new military devices and traitors. Admitting
that Athens had done wrong in oppressing the subject
states in her empire, he asserted that it was nothing compared with Philip's policy of extermination and destruction and his refusal to be at peace with any one except on
a basis of complete domination. And he always remained
loyal to the traditional democratic faith of Athens, which
he had stated in one of his earlier speeches:

> In my opinion it would be better for us to be at war
> with all the states of Greece, provided that they en-
> joyed democratic governments, than to be friends
> with them all if they were ruled by oligarchies; for
> with free states it would not be difficult to make
> peace whenever you wished, but with oligarchical
> governments we could not even form a union on
> which we could rely; for it is not possible that a few
> can entertain friendship for the many, or those who
> exercise arbitrary power for men who choose to live
> on terms of freedom and equality.[2]

"Democracies and dictators cannot exist together," he
declared. "Every dictator is an enemy of freedom."

Aeschines, a more pedestrian mind, was also at first
opposed to Philip, but soon became convinced that opposition was futile and that Athens should make the
best bargain she could. He was used as a tool by Philip,
but Demosthenes' vicious attacks on him as a traitor who

had sold himself were unjustified. Although Philip had bought a few renegade Athenians (one was executed for accepting his money and burning down an arsenal in Athens), Aeschines was undoubtedly a patriot acting in accordance with his belief that the course proposed by Demosthenes was impractical.

Demosthenes won the victory over Aeschines because of his vastly superior oratorical ability and the moral earnestness which he felt and magnificently expressed. Yet, judged by expediency, Aeschines was unquestionably more prudent. Athens lacked the military means, the political vision, and, most of all, the real will to fight, which were required to make resistance successful; nor were the other Greek cities better prepared.

It may be said, and often has been said, that Demosthenes was ill-advised in leading such a forlorn cause; that he looked back to a past that could never be recaptured, that the day of the independent city-state was over, and unification of the Greek world under a powerful ruler was desirable as well as inevitable. It is clear that Demosthenes overestimated the power of Athens and that he exaggerated the malignity of Macedon; Philip was a military autocrat, to be sure, but he respected the culture of the Greek cities, especially Athens, and Alexander the Great was soon to use his military supremacy to do missionary work for that culture. Yet in leading his resistance Demosthenes was true to the finest tradition of his people—the tradition of self-respecting freedom; and if the Greek cities had been sensible enough to follow his advice from the start, the cause might not have been forlorn. And it was by no means inevitable that the unification should come from without, had there been the will and intelligence to achieve it from within.

The fact that his advice was not followed was due to defects in Demosthenes as well as in the people whom he sought to lead. In spite of all his honesty, patriotic fervor, unremitting energy, and oratorical genius, he lacked certain qualities necessary for democratic leadership in times of crisis. He was a prophet rather than a statesman, castigating the Athenian people for their apathy and selfishness, but failing to have the even temper, objective view, and broad human sympathy of Solon and Pericles, or the earthy shrewdness of Cleon, which would have made him effective as a practical politician. He did finally arouse the Athenians, and tried to awaken other states to their peril, but that was not enough. What was needed was a statesman able to foresee and work unceasingly to realize, by conference as well as oratory, the only possible means of successfully resisting Philip: a united front of the most powerful Greek city-states, like the alliance that had opposed Persia at the beginning of the fifth century.

As it was, when Philip finally attacked, Athens and Thebes resisted desperately but were defeated. After the victory of Chaeronea in 338 B.C., Philip adopted a lenient policy toward Athens, partly because it still had a navy that might have been troublesome to him, partly because he had genuine respect for its civilization; but he proceeded to use a strong hand in organizing the Greek world under his control. When he died, Athens pursued the same tactics in its relations to Alexander, at first trying to organize opposition, but finally congratulating him when he captured and destroyed Thebes. The final scene in the drama of Athenian political prestige came when the city made one last attempt to regain her freedom. Her army was crushed, and she had to submit to a temporary loss of her democratic constitution (civic rights were limited by a property qualification), the surrender of her democratic leaders, and the installation of a Macedonian garrison. From this time through the period under Roman domination she was merely a cultural center, continuing to exercise a certain measure of leadership in education, philosophy and the arts.

15

PLATO'S APPRAISAL

Of all the critics of Athenian democracy (and it must be noted that they were themselves a product of the society they criticized), the most severe was Plato; in fact he has often been regarded as the most uncompromising of all foes of democracy. Why he should have had this attitude is not difficult to understand. He came from an aristocratic family; in his youth he had seen his beloved friend and teacher, Socrates, sentenced to death by one of the people's courts; his mind, eager for certainty, was intensely irritated alike by the pragmatic theories of the radical Sophists and the constantly shifting opinions of the Athenian political leaders and the assembly; his taste for grace of living was shocked by the vulgarity of a city overrun with artisans, traders and presumptuous slaves; and his moral code demanded far more than the individualistic hedonism of the Sophists and the standards which were acceptable to the people with whom he was forced to rub shoulders. Furthermore, his youthful ambition for a political career was frustrated when the democracy showed by its treatment of Socrates that it would not acknowledge the sort of leadership he had to offer; and when he turned to the pursuit of philosophy he considered that Athens failed to provide an environment in which his idealism would win proper respect and appreciation.

Yet his philosophy was far from being purely speculative. He was keenly aware of the need of formulating principles that would be socially valuable; he never really lost his political ambition. Starting from Socrates' condemnation of mere opinion as a guide to conduct, he proceeded to construct a theory of knowledge and its application to society which, in his opinion, would remedy the faults of the democratic system in which he lived.

The chief flaws in that system he believed to be the lack of expert intelligence in government and of honest devotion to the public welfare. The use of the lot in selecting officials and the passing of legislation by vote of all the citizens meant that instead of government by specialists, who were equipped for their jobs, the unin-

formed judgment of the least educated citizens had the
most influence; and their leaders, in formulating public
policy, possessed pragmatic opinions but no real knowledge. These so-called statesmen maintained their influence by taxing the rich to provide pleasures for the poor,
with the result that the poor became increasingly idle and
worthless. Instead of asking the advice of authorities in
the science of politics, the people preferred to listen to
orators who flattered them with the aim of gaining success and power for themselves. Our statesmen are experts
in confectionery and dress, he declared, but bad as doc-
tors and gymnastic trainers; "we can point to no one who
has shown himself a good man in the politics of this city."

To the democracy's claims of equality and liberty he
replied that equality is a false conception; men are not
created equal, nor is it just to treat them as if they were.
As for liberty, he granted that a man might do and say
what he wanted to in Athens, and there was some virtue
in that; in the *Laws* he praised the rule of Cyrus of Persia
where the soldiers and generals were treated as equals and
the soldiers fought better because of it, freedom of speech
was permitted so that any man could impart his wisdom
to all, and "the nation progressed in all respects because
there were freedom and friendship and community of
mind among them"; later the Persians declined because
"they diminished the freedom of the people and so destroyed friendship and community of feeling. No city can
be well governed which has not liberty and the alliance
of friendship and wisdom." Yet he believed that the lib-

erty of Athens, which produced "the greatest variety of human nature in what seemed to be the loveliest of states, like an embroidered robe gay with every sort of flower," was not so beautiful after all; lacking a sense of reverent obedience to law, it had degenerated into virtual anarchy, a feverish existence which offered no real good for any one.

So much for the negative criticism of Plato. In the *Republic* he constructed his positive program. It started from a discussion of the nature of justice. The traditional notions that justice consists of "telling the truth and paying one's debts" or "rendering to each man his due," and the two Sophistic theories that it is either a social contract to protect the weak from the strong, or the interest of the stronger, he rejected. We shall best find out what justice is in a community, he said, if we first discover what it is in an individual.

An individual is made up of three elements: appetite, honorable spirit, and reason. He is like a chariot drawn by a powerful but clumsy horse (appetite) and a nervous thoroughbred (honorable spirit), and directed by the charioteer (reason). Justice consists in each one of these fulfilling its proper function and not attempting to do the work of another. Both horses must be kept in healthy condition if the chariot is to get anywhere, for they supply the power, but if the chariot is to avoid being wrecked and is to reach its goal they must be held in check and guided by the charioteer. Appetite and spirit must be controlled by reason.

This analysis he then transferred to the state. In it are the same three elements: appetite, represented by the acquisitive class, the workers and business men, whose primary aim is to get things for themselves; honorable spirit, represented by those who are actuated by motives of public service, the soldiers who sacrifice themselves to guard the community; and reason, represented by the philosophers, who are the most intelligent as well as the most public-spirited members of the community. Justice, here too, consists in each group doing what it is best fitted to do and not attempting to usurp the function of any other group. It is just for the workers to be busy at their jobs and acquire the proper rewards for their work; it is just for the soldiers to win glory in defending their country; it is just for the philosophers to rule. If any one of these tries to do the work better suited to another, especially if a business man, worker, or soldier becomes the ruler, it is unjust to the entire society. For the person whose dominant motive is the acquisition of goods for himself will certainly continue to work for his own interests if he is granted or secures power over his fellow citizens; he has neither the knowledge nor the unselfishness to rule beneficially. Likewise the soldier, no matter how noble his motives may be, is intellectually incapable of directing the policies of the state wisely. Only philosophers should be kings.

Next Plato considered how these classes were to be trained to fulfill their functions and to develop social consciousness. It is the first duty of the state, he said, to establish a system of education which will discover what each child is fitted to do, and then make sure that he is properly trained to do it. Primary education should be the same for all children, controlled by the state and based on the traditional Athenian curriculum: music (and by music Plato meant also literature) and physical training. Aesthetic education he regarded as the very foundation of the good life.

> To us the gods were given as our comrades in the dance, they imparted the delightful sense of rhythm and harmony whereby they cause us to lead our choruses, joining hands in dances and songs. Education is first given through the Muses and Apollo. We must, then, follow the scent like hounds, pursuing beauty of form and melody and song and dance; if these escape us there will be no use in talking about genuine education.[1]

Why is such an education important? Here is Plato's answer:

> A musical education is of the greatest importance, because rhythm and harmony penetrate very deeply to the inward places of the soul and affect it most powerfully, imparting grace; and also because one who has been so trained will perceive most keenly the defects of both art and nature. With true discrimination he will commend and enjoy beautiful objects, and, receiving them into his soul, will grow to be beautiful and good. But shameful things he will properly censure and hate, even in his youth before he is able to understand the reason why; and when reason

comes he will recognize and welcome her in most friendly fashion because of this early training.[2]

In other words, education in the arts develops emotional patterns which influence one's entire life.

But in order to train youth to the sort of emotional reactions that will be socially desirable the material must be carefully selected. Shall men say that a dancer dances and sings well? More than that, they must add "he dances and sings what is good." It is "intolerable and blasphemous" to assert that the function of music is to give pleasure, to be (in Bach's phrase) a pleasant recreation. In an amusing passage in the *Laws* Plato warned against listening to music unaccompanied by words, because it is difficult to recognize the meaning of pure music or to see that any worthy object is represented by it. Music, like every other art, must educate people's moral character.

So there must be strict censorship of the arts. Only those stories and poems which tell of virtuous action, inspiring young people to be brave, sober-minded, truthful and magnanimous, should be permitted. The others must be deleted, "not because they are unpoetical or unattractive to the ear" but because for this very reason they are more likely to have a bad influence. Similarly with music, the effeminate, plaintive and convivial harmonies must be discarded, and only those retained which represent the tones and accents of a brave man, acting with courage, sobriety, and moderation, "the natural rhythms of a well-regulated and manly life."

Consequently artists must be chosen carefully; and if an artist should arrive in the city "so clever as to be able to assume any character and imitate anything," Plato proposed to pay him all respect, but "after pouring perfumed oil upon his head and crowning him with a garland" to send him away to another city. "For ourselves," he declared, "we shall employ for our well-being that more austere and less charming poet who will imitate for us the style of the virtuous man."

> Poets [he concluded] should be compelled to express in their productions the likeness of a good character, and other craftsmen too must be restrained from expressing an evil nature, intemperance, meanness and ungracefulness, whether in the images of living creatures, or buildings, or any other work of their hands. He who is unable to do otherwise shall be forbidden to work in our city, so that our guardians may not be reared among images of evil, as upon unwholesome pastures. We ought rather to seek for artists who desire to track down the nature of the beautiful and graceful, so that our youth, living in a healthful place, may derive good from every side, whence any emanation from beautiful works may strike upon their sight or hearing like a breeze wafting health from kindly lands, and from childhood win them imperceptibly into resemblance, friendship, and harmony with intellectual beauty.[3]

Once these artistic subjects and patterns which have ethical value have been established they must not be changed. Plato abhorred moral innovation. Children, he said, should not be constantly given new games, for then when they grow up they will be always demanding new laws. He praised the Egyptians, who allowed no alterations in their traditional art. "Their ancient sculpture and paintings," he declared exultantly, "are not a whit better or worse than the work of today, but are made with just the same skill. How statesmanlike, how worthy of a legislator!"

Who are to be the censors? Who should make these important decisions? Certainly not the people, for then artists would pander to the public instead of educating them; and "the many are ridiculous in supposing that they know what are proper harmony and rhythm." But neither did Plato delegate the responsibility to any chief of police or self-appointed society to safeguard morals. The best minds are to decide. Philosophers are to be the censors.

Following this elementary education, those who demonstrate that they have the capacity to proceed further should be given training to develop their qualities of courage; the rest will be dismissed to enter the class of artisans and business men. Next, most of those who are pre-eminent in courage will be found unable to profit from advanced intellectual discipline, and they will join the class of soldiers. The few who finally remain will be given a most thorough and exacting training in mathematics and dialectic. Mathematics is important because it gives insight into those principles of harmonious relationships which are so important in regulating a state, and

through dialectic the student comes to arrive at a knowledge of universal concepts which makes government a
science instead of a matter of mere opinion.

Once men are settled in their respective classes, a life
is provided for them in accordance with their needs.
Workers and business men are permitted to live with
their families and secure and hold the private property
which they crave, so long as they show moderation and
do not try to use it to gain power which they do not deserve. But both the soldiers and the philosopher guard-
ians, since they are solely concerned with the welfare of
the community, will own no personal property and have
no family life. Instead, they will live on a communistic
basis which will save them from any temptation to yield
to the desires that dominate the lowest class. The notion
of communism, by the way, was not original with Plato;
Sparta, as we have seen, was a communistic military society, and theories of communism had been advanced in
Athens during the previous century.

This system was not confined by Plato to men. He advocated earnestly that women should be given the same
education and the same opportunities for careers, maintaining that the only difference between men and women
was one of physical strength.

> None of the duties of administering a community be-
> long to woman as woman or to man as man; but
> natural gifts are to be found here and there in both
> sexes alike, and so far as nature is concerned women
> are admissible to all pursuits as well as men.[4]

Even if this system could be put into effect, Plato had no illusions regarding its permanence. His study of history had led him to conclude that social systems tend to deteriorate unless unceasing vigilance constantly re-creates them. Given this aristocracy of intelligence, he foresaw the ambition for personal glory infiltrating among the rulers until it degenerated into timocracy, the rule of those dominated by honorable spirit. These men in turn would be tempted by personal gain and the desire for private property, with the result of oligarchy, rule by the wealthy few who are motivated by their selfish appetites. When their greed became unbridled, it would lead to popular revolt and the installation of democracy. But the majority in their turn would seek merely to satisfy their appetites, conflicts would arise between them and the middle class, until a state of lawlessness and civil war would prevail. This would have to be settled by some authority, and one person would take advantage of the situation to seize power for himself. The tyrant would first gain control by making tempting promises to the people; and he would retain it by maintaining a personal army, confiscating the property of the rich, waging external war to distract attention from the internal problems which he was incapable of solving, getting rid of the associates who helped him attain power, and liquidating anyone who had the intelligence, public spirit, and courage to criticize his conduct or endanger his position. Tyranny, Plato regarded as the worst possible form of government, for it means that one man, governed not by wisdom or standards of honor, but exclusively by his lust for power and personal profit, exercises a whip hand over all the citizens; it is rule, he said, by a mad beast.

In the later part of his life, disillusioned perhaps by the collapse of Sparta, the orderly system of which he admired although he recognized the limitations due to its military policy, and by his own ill-fated attempts to put his ideal state into operation in Syracuse, and favorably impressed by the milder spirit of the Athens of his day, Plato tried in the *Statesman* and the *Laws* to work out a more moderate scheme of government which might actually be put into effect. In the *Statesman* he granted a few practical values to democracy, but still held that its leader should be a wise man who would design the pattern of its policy like a weaver who works without asking the consent of the threads! He contrasted constitutional states, among which he rated monarchy first, aristocracy next, and democracy third, with arbitrary states, among which direct democracy ranked above oligarchy and tyranny. The rule of one man is the most effective, he declared, either for good or bad; the rule of the many is weakest, either for good or bad; so if the choice has to be made, democracy is to be preferred to government by the powerful unscrupulous few or a tyrant.

In the *Laws* he made still further concessions, granting that there was value in giving the ordinary people some voice in their government and the privilege of electing their officials. The best regime Athens ever had, he declared, was in the days when there was a mixed constitution, with a system of classes based on the ownership of property, and liberty disciplined by respect for established law; this was corrupted by the greed of the people for more freedom than they were able to use wisely. He proposed as the best practical set-up a small agricultural city. Private property would be permitted within limits and under public regulation; the rights of property, he declared, were not absolute, but were created by society for its own benefit. Leisure for the citizens was to be secured by having metics do the handicrafts and business and slaves the farming, as in the Spartan system; but the rights of slaves as human beings must be guaranteed by law. There would be monogamous marriage, and women would be expected to participate in public life. Government would be in the hands of all the citizens to the extent of electing the officials, and the final stage of their voting would be by lot, "in order to give the people the sense of equality," but only the two upper property classes would be required to vote; by this device Plato wanted tactfully to discourage the lower classes from engaging in political activity. In such a compromise between oligarchy and democracy, the upper classes would actually do the ruling, but the lower classes would have sufficient political expression to keep them satisfied.

In this treatise Plato went into great detail regarding the laws which should govern the community. In order to give them prestige he wished to put them on a religious basis, with the sanction of Apollo, the god dearest to aristocrats. Most interesting is his analysis of criminal

law, in which he advanced the theory that crime is a dis-
ease, and the laws should act as wise parents rather than
oppressive masters, attempting to heal the offender both
for his sake and that of society. Among capital offenses
he listed religious agnosticism. Education was to include
universal training under state control for girls as well as
boys, the teachers being aliens, since no citizen would de-
mean himself by such craftsmanship any more than he
would by engaging in manual labor.

The foreign relations of this state were to be governed
by the principle of making alliances with other Greek
states so as to guarantee security from barbarian aggression. Plato visualized Greece as a society of friendly states
with a common code of international law which would
outlaw warfare between them. This was a step beyond the
current Greek practice of one alliance attempting to hold
another in check, which had regularly resulted in war, but
it was not a sufficient solution; practical politicians planned
better than Plato in this respect, as we shall see, when
they created genuine confederations of Greek states.

Plato appraised democracy. How shall democracy ap-
praise him? First it must grant that he was much more of
a democrat than has been usually admitted. He recognized many of the psychological needs of individuals and
tried to meet them; he held that people err because of
ignorance and commit crime because they are diseased,
and should be taught and cured rather than punished; he
advocated a system of universal education under state
control, to discover and develop the capacities of each

child regardless of wealth or birth; he argued that women should have opportunities for careers on the same basis as men; and he visualized a society whose aim should be the common good and in which every person should do the work and win the rewards that his abilities merited.

Yet it is true that in background, temperament and conviction Plato was an aristocrat. He had little confidence in the intellectual capacity of the ordinary man or his ability to rise above selfish interests to take a conscious part in promoting the social purposes of the entire community. Most men he considered so lacking by nature in intellectual and spiritual qualities that they were fit for little except manual labor and mercantile pursuits, both of which Plato considered inferior occupations. Education was to be available to all, but the material presented was to be censored by the best minds; the people were to be allowed to know only what their rulers thought best, and were to have no share in formulating the curriculum or determining the purposes of education. Finally, the most anti-democratic attitude of all, the society Plato desired was to be a static one. Men were restricted to fixed functional groups for life, institutions and laws were to be unchanging, and stability established by a few was regarded as superior to evolution through the co-operation of many.

16

THE POLITICAL
SCIENCE OF
ARISTOTLE

No creator of Utopias, but a keen-minded biologist who classified governments as coolly as he did marine life, Aristotle had nevertheless an aristocratic background like that of his teacher, Plato; his disciplined mind reacted in many ways like Plato's to the disorders that he had seen in the Athenian democracy; and he, too, craved a society that would be static enough to permit a scientist and philosopher like himself to work in peace and quiet. But he was very much a realist; he showed greater tolerance for the actual governments which he studied, and realized that they met the practical needs of different sorts of people. His *Politics* is an invaluable study of the virtues and defects of those various systems.

"Man is by nature a social and political animal," he declared. The satisfying of material needs led men at first to congregate in communities, but their association in states came to meet their deeper needs for a good life. Only as members of states can men succeed in realizing their complete potentialities.

The forms of states which have developed, Aristotle classified under three broad headings, recognizing that there have been many varieties within each group: monarchy, aristocracy, and democracy. Monarchy, if the ruler were intelligent and unselfish, he regarded as the best form of government; the head of it could take prompt action to secure orderly procedure and create harmonious relations between his subjects. But this condition he granted was ideal rather than real. Once unlimited power was in the hands of one man, the tendency was for it to degenerate into government for the selfish interests of the ruler and become tyranny, which Aristotle condemned without qualification as the worst form of government. Even if the tyrant by the use of his superior force, the army and secret police, keeps his subjects unable or afraid to revolt and thus succeeds in maintaining order, by destroying their initiative he makes the state unproductive; and there is always the likelihood that the sparks among those who feel the injustice of their welfare being sacrificed to the profit of one man will flame into revolution.

And revolution, according to Aristotle, is the greatest political evil.

The same may be said of aristocracy. Theoretically it is good to have the government in the hands of the wisest and most public-spirited men; they can act more efficiently than a great number, and have the advantage of representing more varied judgments and interests than those of a single man. But actually when power gets in the control of any single group those men also tend to use it for their own interests. So aristocracy degenerates into oligarchy, which likewise leads to discontent and revolt on the part of the mass of the people. Whether these oligarchies are based on birth or wealth, they are equally unstable. If they are kept static by military means, they are effective only in so far as there are conditions of war; "like iron that is not used they lose their edge in times of peace; the citizens have never been taught how to live a peaceful life."

So we come to Aristotle's appraisal of democracy. Theoretically inferior to monarchy and aristocracy, a democratic system (with certain very definite limitations) appeared to him actually the most satisfactory form of community organization.

The basis of democracy, he declared, is the distribution of offices and rewards on a basis of the equality of individuals, and personal liberty for all. This he believed was founded on a sound evaluation of human nature. The collective judgment may be expected to be superior to that of any single individual or group, for while some people see one aspect of a problem, some another, all combined see every aspect. Even in judging works of art the opinion of many men may be trusted more than that of a teacher of art or the artist himself. The collective honesty is likewise superior, because it is concerned with community goods. Furthermore, people become educated to public responsibility by sharing in public office, by joining in deliberation with regard to policy, and by electing their officials. And men find more satisfaction and work better when they do what they like and live as they please.

Yet, granting all this, Aristotle believed that democracy must be saved from degenerating into demagogy. When the majority rules, that majority inevitably consists of the lower economic class. It, too, will tend to legislate exclusively in its own interest. So the will of the common people must be held in check by a constitution which establishes a government of laws above that of men; "men should not think it slavery to live according to the rule of a constitution, for it is their salvation." (One is reminded of William Penn's Frame of Government: "Any government is free to the people under it, whatever be the Frame, where the laws rule and the people are a party to these laws.")

Aristotle accordingly rated as best among the various types of democracy that which functions in a society where the common people find it inconvenient to express their will very much, specifically in agricultural communities where the farmers cannot take time to attend many assembly meetings and are kept busy and contented enough so that they will not bother to vote. Then government will be entrusted for the most part to the wealthier and abler middle-class people who have the leisure to take part in politics. When trade and commerce bring their explosive elements into the civic picture (Aristotle, like his fellow aristocrats, had little love for trade and commerce), the best constitution is one which establishes a property qualification for public service, provides no pay for officials, and allows the people merely to review the acts of their magistrates. Here Aristotle was looking back wistfully to the time of Solon. If all the people must participate, at least their power in assembly should be limited by law. Finally, he declared, there is pure democracy (like that of the Athens of his day), in which the people have complete and immediate legislative power. This he considered the worst form of democracy, a government of men rather than of laws.

In spite of his theoretical recognition of the corporate virtues of common men, Aristotle was too much of an aristocrat to have much faith in their wisdom or unselfishness on any given occasion. When the lower classes make the decisions without restriction, he said, they disregard the rights of minorities, tax the wealthy few unfairly, and are the prey of demagogues, their own party leaders. "Such a government will have many supporters," he added drily, "for most people prefer to live in a disorderly rather than a sober way." But even such a system he admitted, with an eye on Athens, could function fairly well, so long as the people had sufficient sense to be reasonable toward minorities and not pamper the poor to the extent of destroying their initiative and sense of public duty.

A government of laws: what did Aristotle consider such a society to be? One in which the ruling power is restrained from taking advantage of any minority group, where a spirit of moderation and conciliation governs all classes in their dealings with one another, where the acquisition of private or group gains at the expense of the rest of the people is prohibited. This condition is most likely to exist when there is a large and powerful middle class. Such a class holds in check the selfishness of the very rich and the envy of the very poor, and is reasonable in its own demands since it embodies that golden mean whereby states as well as individuals "pass through life in safety."

So far Aristotle judged various types of states on the basis of their actual experience as he had observed it. But, like Plato, he was interested primarily not in the machinery of government but in the purposes of government, which, like Plato, he visualized as chiefly educational and moral. What end does government serve? The end of creating for all of its citizens a good life, a life rich in cultural activity, reasonable, unselfish, and happy. Only a few, he considered, could meet the tests he set up for the magnanimous man, but every society should aim to make this group as large as the capacities of men would allow. Within the state many associations on a lesser scale will make their contributions to this richness of experience, but the state will unite all of them into the supreme association which guarantees justice and stimulates brotherhood; justice which assures each member his rights and exacts from each his due; friendship which makes living together the generous sharing of a common life. By this means the final goal will be attained: the happiness of each member of the community and of the community as a whole.

Finally Aristotle outlined his idea of a satisfactory state, which is a much less pretentious one than Plato's Republic. It will be a community limited in size, large enough to be self-sufficient but small enough so that the people will know each other and be able to judge their officials from actual contact with them. There will be slaves and aliens in it to do the required manual labor, for such work is unworthy of citizens; private property will be permitted, since it encourages individual initiative and makes possible the generosity which Aristotle believed especially desirable in his ideal man, but there will also be sufficient common property to develop a sense of public responsibility; the young will be organized into an army to wage war, when war is required, and the governing will be in the hands of the older men who are more experienced; all citizens will have some share in the exercise of power, but there will be distinctions in rewards based on ability; universal education for the citizens will train the will and the moral and aesthetic sense as well as the intelligence of the young, so that they can make their contribution to the social welfare.

It is likely that Aristotle was influenced by Pericles' ideal for Athens in formulating this state. A comparison with Pericles' program reveals many points of similarity. But he was much less democratic than Pericles. He was distrustful of the soundness of the people's judgment. He disliked the mercantile and artisan classes, and regarded artisans and business men as means whereby the leisurely few could attain a life of distinction. Women he believed were essentially inferior to men, deficient in both physical and mental strength; their virtues, he said, were "temperance, and a love—but not a sordid one—of work"! He refused slaves any economic and social rights as human beings, considering them to be sub-men who lack the capacity of reason; "that some should rule and others be ruled is both expedient and right; at birth some are marked for slavery, others for mastery." And he had no solution to offer of the major problem of the Greek cities, the chief cause of unrest and revolution: the constant wars and the inability to create a co-operative society of states.

We may conclude that Aristotle set in sharp relief democracy's fundamental philosophy and appreciated some of its virtues as well as its defects. The chief weakness of his political theory lay in his failure to consider democracy as a dynamic organism rather than a static system. Many of the elements which Aristotle condemned as disorderly were actually the signs of healthy activity, and were part of the process whereby the people were achieving their education and making social progress.

17

U N I O N   T H E N

We have already seen how ineffective was the constantly changing network of alliances by which the separate Greek states tried to protect themselves against one another and against enemies from outside Greece, and how the final result was submission to the unified military power of Macedon and of Rome. We have seen how equally unavailing were attempts at domination by any one Greek state: Athens, Sparta, Thebes, because of the mutual jealousy between the Greek cities and the lack of sufficient military strength or political sagacity on the part of any one of them to create an enduring empire. But some Greeks tried to solve the problem in another and more promising way: by federations of free states, in which the organizing principle was one of co-operation. Unfortunately these attempts were never made on a large enough scale or under competent enough leadership to give them the prestige and power required for great success; but the fact that they were made at all and had even limited success is one of the most significant creative achievements of Greek politics. Perhaps it is the most important one for us today.

The earliest venture in federation was the Amphictyonic League, formed originally by a group of cities in Thessaly. We know little about its organization, but one of the policies first agreed upon by its members was not to cut off the running-water supply of any other member. At the beginning of the sixth century B.C., this league became prominent by helping Delphi conduct a successful war to control the valuable orchard environs of the religious sanctuary of Apollo. Shortly after this the league took over the direction of the Pythian games, which, like those at Olympia, were among the most effective international agencies in the Greek world; there, whatever wars were raging, state officials, athletes, artists and ordinary citizens met every four years under terms of truce, exchanged views, settled differences, and got to know one another better. Later the Amphictyonic League included many other states of Greece in a loosely knit confederation for the purpose of regulating the laws governing Delphi and for protecting the shrine. Finally, in the fourth century B.C., in consequence of the Phocians securing control of Delphi, Philip of Macedon was asked to help dislodge them, and with his coming the autonomy which the separate states had previously enjoyed was doomed.

A second attempt at confederation was the Delian League, organized for protection against Persia. In its early stages it was, as we have seen, a genuine league of autonomous states, with a common navy, treasury and legal system. But the superior power of Athens led to its transformation into an empire. If Athens had had the wisdom to restrain her ambition and be content with economic and cultural penetration, chances were good that this league might have been a permanent influence in stabilizing and strengthening Greek interstate relations. But the opportunity was thrown away at that time, and later, when Athens reorganized the league on a smaller scale with a more democratic constitution, again aggressive ambition ruined it.

Similar federations of states in the Peloponnesus and Boeotia came to a similar end, owing to domination by the city which had the greatest military power. In 505 B.C., a league was formed embracing a majority of the states in the Peloponnesus; theoretically the members were bound to abide by decisions adopted by a majority vote, but the sessions of the league were held in Sparta and her military leadership made her virtually an autocratic master. The Boeotian League, organized in the fifth century, brought several cities of that area into a federal union; they had representation in the council in proportion to their military strength. But here again the superiority of Thebes reduced the league to an alliance controlled by its most powerful member.

An attempt to realize the dream of Isocrates—a union of all the leading Greek states to oppose Persia—was made under the direction of Philip of Macedon. At the Congress of Corinth a constitution was drawn up providing that each city retain its existing constitution, that intercity disputes be referred to a Panhellenic court, and that the freedom of the seas be guaranteed to all members. Philip ostensibly demanded only that cities should pledge themselves not to furnish aid to any foreign power hostile to him. But this, too, was autocracy masquerading as federation. Philip had an iron hand within his velvet glove. Once it was organized, he dictated to the league his plan for a united offensive against Persia. It was voted, although without enthusiasm; the cities had little confidence in their self-appointed leader or affection for him. How well he understood their attitude is evidenced by his establishing Macedonian garrisons at key points throughout Greece. But the plan was never put into operation by Philip; he was murdered before the campaign started. Alexander inherited his leadership of the confederacy, but he also met with little enthusiasm. During his campaign to consolidate his power nearer home the Greek cities began to negotiate with Persia, and Thebes openly rebelled. Alexander acted promptly to

defeat the rebel city, and by vote of the confederacy utterly destroyed it and enslaved the surviving inhabitants.
There was no real debate over this policy as there was in
Athens after the revolt of Mitylene. With Alexander at
its head the federation was never more than a rubber
stamp for its master.

Four other federations succeeded in a modest fashion
in realizing actual union. In Chalcidice early in the fourth
century a group of cities was organized by Olynthus, a
flourishing commercial center, into a federation which
functioned well for a brief time. It provided that citizens
in every state of the union had full rights of citizenship
in every other state, and Olynthus was wise enough not
to assume special privileges for itself. Under this arrangement local rivalries were overcome and a spirit of cordial
co-operation prevailed. But further development was
made impossible by the reluctance of neighboring cities
to yield their sovereignty and by the determined opposition of Sparta, which preferred disunity throughout the
Greek world to any combinations of states.

Following the defeat of Sparta by Thebes, a group of
Arcadian cities formed a federal union to guarantee future
protection against Sparta. Its constitution was modeled
on the democratic pattern, with an assembly consisting
of all the citizens of the federated states to pass on matters of common policy and a representative council of fifty
members with executive functions. At first Thebes was
sympathetic to this federation as a means of checking
Spartan ambition, and supported it even to the extent of

invading Spartan territory. The league continued, allying itself with various Greek states in the characteristic fourth-century game of maintaining a balance of power, until Macedonian control finally reduced it to impotence.

More lasting was the Aetolian League, composed of a group of cities in northwestern Greece, which likewise established relations of non-aggression among themselves and framed an admirable constitution, according to which each city retained its local autonomy but united with the others for the protection of their mutual interests. At the beginning the making of decisions rested in an assembly open to the citizens of all the states, which met twice yearly; administration was in the hands of a council chosen from the cities in proportion to their military strength. Later, as the league grew in membership and extent of territory, a small standing committee was elected annually to decide on questions of policy, and a financial board was elected to manage the funds. The chief executive officers, a president and commanding general, were elected yearly and were not eligible for immediate re-election. In this way there was considerable flexibility and a fair distribution of offices among the various cities in the confederation.

Unfortunately, however, the same wisdom was not applied in their relations with their neighbors. In the third century the league became aggressive and began a program of military expansion. After forming alliances with cities in central Greece it sent an army into the Peloponnesus, and it entered into an alliance with the Roman commander Titus Quinctius Flamininus when he made his successful campaign against Macedon. Later, however, the Aetolians led a revolt against Rome, charging that the autonomy promised by Rome meant "better polished, but heavier, chains," and allied itself with Antiochus III of Syria. The victory of Rome led to the dissolution of the league.

Clearly this league fell into the characteristic pitfall of the separate Greek states: it failed to apply its sound principles of local government to its foreign relations; its ambition for territorial expansion involved it in ill-advised alliances; the consequence was its downfall.

The most promising Greek effort toward federation was made by a group of cities in the Peloponnesus. The Achaean League, an association of twelve states which had functioned quietly for some time before the conquest of Alexander the Great, was reorganized on a firmer basis at the start of the third century to deal with Alexander's successors in Macedon, Asia Minor, and Egypt, and to provide protection from aggression. Its double aim was to guarantee its members local autonomy and security from external threats. For this purpose a common army and courts were created, common currency and weights and measures were adopted, and policies were decided by a representative council which met twice a year or more often when circumstances required it. The membership of this council included men from all the cities, elected annually; the voting was done by cities, and a majority vote decided all matters which were brought up, including declarations of war and treaties of peace. There were several minor officials, but the chief executive officer, elected annually by the council, was a general. The reason for this is obvious: the league had to spend most of its energy and resources in repelling attacks. If it had not been compelled to do this it might have been able to extend the confederation to include a good part of the Greek world, but it never had a fair chance. An attempt was made by General Aratus to expel Macedon from Greece and re-establish freedom for all the Greek cities, but his generalship was not equal to his statesmanship, and even that was not astute enough to deal with the jealous Greek states and the hungry wolves beyond Greece. He got financial aid from Egypt; he even won support at one time from the Aetolian League; but Athens refused to co-operate with him, and ultimately, when he forced Sparta to join at the tragic expense of betraying a league member to Macedon, the federation came under Macedon's control. It never thereafter exercised more than local influence.

The pattern is one with which we have now become only too familiar: a promising organization of states wrecked on the reefs of jealousies and ambitions and the lack of foresight and leadership necessary to induce enough other cities to join on a co-operative basis.

The historian of the Achaean League was Polybius, one of the thousand Achaeans sent to Rome as hostages after the battle of Pydna in 168 B.C. His father had spent much of his life as a leading official of the league, and

Polybius himself had been in its service. During his stay
in Rome he won the favor of his conquerors and was
employed by them in their diplomatic dealings with
Greece. He became convinced that the Romans were
destined to rule, and he wrote in praise of a mixed constitution such as he conceived the Roman one to be, including kingly, aristocratic and democratic elements, because he believed such a system of checks and balances
was the best guarantee of preserving law and order.

With abortive democratic revolts in the Greek states
he had no sympathy; his own admiration was for the stability enforced by Rome. Yet enough of his youthful loyalty remained for him to appreciate, perhaps over-gener-
ously, the real contribution that the Achaean League had
made. It was, he declared, a very remarkable political
union, the first instance of cities overcoming their conflicts of interest by creating a co-operative society, a single commonwealth, which was joined by neighboring
states when they realized how conducive membership was
to community welfare; "nowhere could be found a purer
principle and practice of equality, freedom of speech, and,
in a word, true democracy, than among the Achaeans."

He described its early reputation for honorable dealing;
how when civil war broke out in Magna Graecia the
cities there brought in representatives of the Achaean
League as mediators, and formed a league of their own
on the same principles; and again, after the battle of
Leuctra the victorious Thebans referred matters in dis-
pute to the Achaeans for settlement, since "the Achaeans,

although not powerful, were famous for their trustworthiness and high character."

Polybius also pictured the difficulties facing a high-minded statesman like Aratus, who had to deal with autocrats; "he knew that kings do not regard any one as their natural foe or friend, but measure enmity and friendship by only one standard—expediency." And in these noble words he expressed the conviction of the Achaean League as well as his own:

> That war is terrible I admit, but it is not so terrible that we should submit to anything in order to avoid it. Why do we boast of our civic equality and freedom of speech and all that we mean by the word liberty, if nothing is preferable to peace? Peace, with justice and honor, is the most beautiful and profitable of possessions, but if it is allied with baseness and cowardice nothing is more shameful and disastrous.[1]

The aim of the Achaean League was a worthy one; the procedures were wise; and the courage with which the attempt at federal union was made deserves all our praise. But its political and military strength was pitifully inadequate to deal with the menace that came, first from Macedon, and then from Rome.

18

INDIVIDUAL LIBERTY

AND WORLD-PATRI-

OTISM

In a world where the cities in which men had been educated to versatile and responsible citizenship had been
crushed and where ordinary men had been robbed of
their political initiative, first by the superior military
power of Macedon and finally by the might of Rome,
where was freedom any longer to be found?

The answer was the same as many of the old nobility
had given when democracy deprived them of their prestige and influence in former days: in the anodynes of individual pleasure and self-respect. But now these consola-

tions were rationalized into systems of practical philosophy which saved those who believed in them from a sense of futility and gave them a measure of happiness.

To great numbers of people Epicurus provided this satisfaction. In the third century B.C., he established a community in Athens known as the Garden, where he lived with disciples who included women and slaves. He was a kindly man in his attitude toward all people; he sought no luxuries and no renown, content if in simple ways he could achieve happiness. For pleasure, he said, following the doctrine of the radical Sophists, is the aim of every man. But it is not enough to say simply that; we must go on to determine what are the most enduring and qualitatively best pleasures. Sound sense tells us that they are found in friendship with kindred souls ("Friendship dances through the world, summoning us to happiness"), the appreciation of lovely things, the doing of just actions, the satisfying of normal desires.

In our relations with our fellow men we shall fail to realize the serenity of mind which is the fruit of such experience, Epicurus said, if we desire possessions which are outside of our control. One must learn to be content with a few simple and natural pleasures ("There is honor in simple poverty"). Since political ambition deals with rewards in the power of other men to give or deny, it must be avoided.

But the chief obstacle in the way of happiness is the fear men have of what the gods will do to them and of death. Those fears are unreasonable, Epicurus said.

There are doubtless gods, but they live a detached life of their own, with no concern about us; and each person is a fortuitous concourse of atoms which will be dispersed when death comes. "So death, which is regarded as the most terrible of evils, is of no concern to us; for while we exist, death is not, and when death comes, we are not."

Justice was defined by Epicurus as a compromise of self-interest, made in order that both parties may avoid injury; by social contract we should not deprive other people of their possessions, because if we do they might take away ours. But here again one must not be troubled about what others do; the secret of happiness is to expect little of fortune, to be fortified inwardly against any circumstance. Self-sufficiency is the means by which one wins security and peace of mind. So freedom, popularly defined as the ability to get what one wants, to the Epicureans was rather the ability to want what one gets. Although their leader had simple tastes, his followers were for the most part people who had a fair share of the world's goods to enjoy; and this is a limitation of the Epicurean philosophy, that few men, until they are free from want, will be able to profit from such consolation.

Another practical faith, first stated by Antisthenes in the fifth century B.C., became known as Cynicism ("a dog's life") because its enemies considered that the Cynics lived like dogs. They, too, believed that self-sufficiency was the one desirable goal, but in order to achieve it not even the goods and human relations required by the Epicureans were needed; a man must be dependent on no external things: class, property, fame, or even the pleasure and learning that come from association with other people. Five things greater than the Persian Empire, one of them declared, are Wisdom, Self-Sufficiency, Truth, Candor, and Freedom. Once a man possesses these he has everything, and he can achieve them by himself.

So they lived in the simplest possible way, eating the plainest food, drinking only water, wearing one garment all the year around, and exposing themselves to every kind of weather. Why are men sick and unhappy? they asked. Because they weaken themselves with rich food and drink and luxurious living, worry about getting and keeping possessions, "live herded in cities in order to be safe, then proceed to injure one another as if they had gotten together for that purpose."

The most picturesque of the Cynics was Diogenes, a fourth-century Athenian. Many stories are told which illustrate his pungent wit. Reproached at being condemned to exile by the people of Sinope, he snapped back, "And I condemn them to stay in Sinope." Seeing servants carrying a load of furniture, he said, "Isn't their master ashamed to be ruler of all this but not of himself?" Again, when he saw a child drinking with its hands, he threw away his cup, saying, "A child has gone me one better in the simple life." Asked what wine he liked best, he replied, "Other people's." Seen begging before a statue, he explained, "I am learning how to meet with refusal." "It is the mark of God," he declared, "to need nothing, and of those who are like God to need little."

Along with their contempt for material possessions they also hated pretense and pride. The story is told of Diogenes that he walked about Athens during the day with a lighted lamp, trying to find a real man; when asked where in Greece he had met men of this sort, he answered, "Nowhere—but I found some children in Sparta." When he saw richly dressed young Rhodians at Olympia he laughed and said, "Pride!"; then, seeing Spartans clad in their shabby and filthy smocks, he said, "Also pride!" One of the Cynics, seeing a man pleased with the handsome cloak he was wearing, fingered it and said, "A sheep used to wear this—and kept on being a sheep." Diogenes, when asked how a man can become master of himself, replied, "By applying to himself the criticism he makes of others."

But such incidents as these do not indicate how deeply the Cynics probed below the surface of human customs and prejudices. They made a radical attack on many fundamental beliefs. They declared that marriage was an absurd convention; love should be a free matter of consent. They ridiculed the religion of the people. When Diogenes saw a man admiring the votive offerings dedicated by men who had escaped shipwreck, he said, "There would have been many more if we had the offerings of those who didn't escape"; when asked for an offering to Cybele, Great Mother of the gods, Antisthenes replied, "Don't expect any contribution from me. It is the gods' duty to support their mother." Patriotism they also regarded as unreasonable. Since one man is by nature like another, no matter where he lives, he should be bound to no community. Asked what was his city, Diogenes replied, "I am a citizen of the world."

This simple and, on the whole, negative attitude was translated into more positive terms by the Stoics. The founder of this faith was Zeno, a merchant from Cyprus who began his teaching at the end of the fourth century B.C. He agreed with the Cynics that externals are not important (although he did not scorn them, as Diogenes had done), that distinctions of wealth and social class are to be disregarded, and that men are brothers in the great city of the world. "All men," he said, "should be considered as our fellow citizens, there should be one way of life, one order like that of a single flock feeding on a common pasture." But he developed a philosophy that went far beyond the naturalism of the Cynics. According to him there is in the universe the animating force of Reason, and every individual shares in this universal principle by virtue of the reason that is within him. His object in life should be to free his reason from the physical desires that prevent it from achieving perfect harmony with its divine source; in that harmony, regardless of the circumstances of life, he finds freedom.

In practical terms the Stoics followed the precepts of the Cynics, that happiness is attained by self-sufficiency, that material goods and rewards must be regarded with indifference. But here, too, they had a more positive program. They recognized the fact that men must learn to live together helpfully in communities, and that as members of society they have duties to fulfill toward their fellow men. A world organization was their ideal; but failing that they believed that mixed constitutions of the Aristotelian type were most satisfactory.

The Stoic doctrine became the leading personal guide of life throughout the Roman Empire, the chief faith that offered men the sense of controlling their own destinies when one powerful state could dictate the conditions of their lives.

Epictetus, a slave living in Rome in the first century A.D., made the most eloquent statement of this creed. "Many people have said," he declared, "that only the free are to be educated; but wise men say, Only the educated are free." What is this education? First, the realization that the world is governed by Universal Reason, in which we all share because it is within every one of us. This we must cultivate; and to cultivate it no external goods are required, only a reasonable attitude of will; in fact external things are dangerous because they divert us from the one necessary aim of our lives. "Remember this, that it is not only desire of office and property that debases men and makes them subservient to others, but also desire of peace and leisure and travel and learning. Devotion to any external thing makes you subservient to some one else." But when we live in accordance with reason we are no longer ruled by desire, we cease feeling insecure, dissatisfied and fearful, we attain the supreme happiness of freedom.

> He is free whom nothing can hinder, who has things at his disposal as he wishes. But the man who can be hindered or compelled or involved in anything against his will is a slave. And who is he whom nothing can hinder? The man who aims at nothing which is not his own. And what are the things that are not our own? Everything which is not under our control, either to have or not to have, or to have of a certain quality or under certain conditions. So the body is not our own, nor is our property our own. If, then, you passionately desire one of these things as though it were yours, you will deservedly pay the price of one who aims at what does not belong to him. The road which leads to freedom, the only release from slavery, is to be able to say at all times with your whole heart,

> Lead thou me on, O Zeus and Destiny,
> Where from of old it was decreed for me.[1]

So men must not be troubled over their station in life, or their health, possessions, or reputation, realizing that all of these are beyond their control. "Remember that you are an actor in a play, which the Playwright plots as he wishes. It is your business simply to act well the rôle assigned to you; the selection of the cast is Another's."

Everything which is considered a misfortune should be regarded as a challenge not to be affected by it. Nor is even death to be feared.

You have received everything, even your very self, from Another. Do you complain, then, and criticize the Giver if he takes something away from you? Who are you, and for what purpose have you come into the world? Did He not bring you here? Did He not show you the light? Has He not given you fellow-workers, and your perceptions and your reason? And as what did He give you life? Was it not as a mortal, one to live on earth with a little portion of flesh and for a time to see His governance and partake with Him in His pageant and festival? Are you not willing, then, as long as it has been granted you, to look at the pageant and the festival, and then, when He leads you forth, to go with an obeisance and thanks to Him for what you have heard and seen?

As for me, I would wish death to overtake me while I am occupied with nothing but my moral will, trying to make it tranquil, unhindered, unconstrained, free. This is what I would be engaged in when death finds me, so that I can say to God, "Have I transgressed Thy commands? Have I in any way misused the resources which Thou didst give me? Have I ever accused Thee or criticized Thy governance? I fell sick when it was Thy will; so did others, but I willingly. I became poor when Thou didst will it, but joyously. I never held office, in accordance with Thy will; I never desired office. Hast Thou ever seen me despondent for that reason? Have I not always come into Thy presence with a cheerful face, ready for any of Thy commands? Now it is Thy will that I leave the festival. I depart, giving all thanks to Thee because Thou didst regard me as worthy to share Thy festival and see Thy works and understand Thy governance." [2]

Epictetus was friendly toward his fellow men, considering them his kin, and was eager to help them outgrow their mistaken judgments and their fears. We should not be angry with those who do evil, he said, but rather pity them.

> If the greatest misfortune that can happen to any one is the loss of what is most important, and a right moral will is the most important, is it not enough for a man to lose this without enduring your anger besides? If you must have unnatural feelings when a man suffers misfortune, pity him, do not hate him; give up such an attitude of hostility and hatred; do not say as the spiteful multitude do: "Those accursed and abominable fools!" [3]

Yet, however much one helps those who are unhappy and in error, they must never be sympathized with to the extent of disturbing one's own equanimity.

> If a man is unfortunate, remember that he alone is to blame for his misfortune; for God created all men for happiness and tranquillity of mind, as was natural for Him to do who cares for us and protects us like a father.[4]

Nor should the Stoic be concerned with politics.

> Are you looking for more important politics than that which he practices now? Shall he come forward in the Athenian assembly and discuss incomes and revenues, when he ought to be talking with all

men, Athenians, Corinthians and Romans alike, not about revenues or income, peace or war, but about happiness and unhappiness, about slavery and freedom? When a man is practicing such important politics do you ask me if he is to be a politician? Ask me also if he will hold office, and I will say again, what office is greater than that which he now has?

In the case of kings and tyrants, their armed bodyguard enables them to censure and punish people, even though they themselves are wicked; but the wise man's conscience gives him this authority, he needs no arms or bodyguard. When he sees that he has watched over men and labored for their good, and that all his thoughts have been those of a friend and servant of the gods, why should he not with confidence speak freely to his brothers, his children, his kinsmen in humanity?

Reviling, blows, insults, mean nothing to him. For he realizes that the inferior must of necessity yield to the superior, and that his body is physically inferior to the physically superior crowd. So he never enters this contest in which he can be beaten, but immediately resigns what is not his own. But when it is a question of his own moral will, no one can rob him of that or master it.[5]

How shall we judge this freedom of the Stoics in terms of the democratic way of life? The principles that men must be educated to make reasonable judgments in order to be truly free; that all men are brothers, with responsibilities to help one another beyond any limits of class or country; that property values are insignificant in comparison with human ones; and that the spirits of men must overcome insecurity and fear, all are sound doctrines of democracy. But the Stoic means of achieving these principles seem inadequate. They offer refuge from the physical wants and the social restrictions imposed on men by positing a universal justice which seems very far away from the actual conditions of human living that need to be improved; and in the glad submission to this universal principle one may see an emotional sublimation of the submission which has to be made to earthly rulers. If men believe that every one should be content with his lot and seek only peace of mind in subservience to the will of God, for all their ideals of personal duty to others in the brotherhood of man they cannot be counted on to wage a very determined battle for justice in the society in which they live. It is a creed of escapism.

Yet it was a noble escapism; the serenity attained involved, not surrender to men, but dignity and courage; the Stoic as an individual made no compromise with tyranny. Epictetus tells this story of a Roman senator who put his Stoic faith into practice:

The Emperor Vespasian sent word to Priscus Helvidius, forbidding him to attend a meeting of the Senate. Priscus replied, "You can keep me from being a senator, but as long as I am one I must come to the meeting." "Very well, then," said Vespasian, "come, but do not speak." "If you do not ask for my opinion I shall not speak." "But as head of the Senate I have to ask it." "And I have to say what I think right." "If you do I shall have you put to death." "Did I ever tell you," said Priscus, "that I was immortal? You will do your part, and I mine. It is yours to kill, mine to die without flinching; yours to banish, mine to go into exile without grieving."

What good did Priscus do, you ask, one man against the Emperor? What good does the purple do to the garment, except to have its own distinction as purple and to be an example of beauty to others? [6]

Yes, even when the Roman Emperor asserted his autocratic power and had Priscus Helvidius killed, he could not take away his subject's essential liberty or self-respect. Who can believe that the ultimate victory was Vespasian's? As long as this individual devotion to freedom and honor remained, the germ of democracy lived.

Conclusion

LOOKING FORWARD

JUDGING FREEDOM TO BE HAPPINESS, AND
COURAGE TO BE THE CREATOR OF FREEDOM,
IT REMAINS FOR YOU NOT TO FEAR ANY
RISKS, BUT TO RIVAL WHAT THESE MEN
HAVE DONE.   —*Pericles*

After surveying the evolution of Greek democracy it may
be that we shall arrive at a final mood of pessimism, because efforts which accomplished so much were dissipated
in wars and ultimately suppressed by autocratic military
power. But such a conclusion is far from justified.

It must be remembered that these were the first experiments in democratic institutions and their control.
When we realize that in spite of all the inexperience
within and constant attack from without, Athens created
and maintained for so long a time one of the greatest

civilizations in the history of the world, we have a right to feel confidence rather than despair in the possibilities of democracy.

And if men learn anything from the experience of the past, we can profit from studying the causes of its decline. From an economic point of view the Greeks always lived in a world of scarcity, where conflict for the possession of limited resources led to internal strife, in which personal and group interests were often placed ahead of community ones, and external aggression led to war. Their conception of political democracy was a partial one, not extending to women, aliens or slaves within the state or relations with other states, hence huge resources of cooperative energy, devotion to the common good, and potential leadership were left untapped. Both rival alliances of states and imperial domination encouraged rather than prevented conflict. Experiments in federal organization were effective for a time, but were conducted on too small a scale to be permanently successful; and any large scale was next to impossible because of inadequate communication facilities. This economic and political situation resulted in revolutions and wars which exhausted the resources of the Greek world, sapped its morale, and finally led to its becoming the victim of autocratic enemies.

Have we reason to believe that modern democracies can master such difficulties? There is cause for confidence. Science has now given us the prospect of an economy of abundance, which, if properly distributed, will make it unnecessary for any group to seek prosperity at the expense of its neighbors. It has also provided means of communication which make the democratic process workable on a larger scale than at any previous time. We have a conception of democracy, however imperfectly realized, which is much more inclusive than the Athenian one, and universal education makes available human resources, loyalties, and leadership which have never yet been given an adequate opportunity to make their contribution to the common welfare. But the greatest reason for hope lies in the possibility of international co-operation among free peoples to eliminate authoritarian aggression and war. Our techniques of organization within a democracy have been developed to the point where we may believe they can be applied with equal success on an international scale. Certainly no other solution seems to offer any prospect of enduring peace; control by one dominant nation, imperial rivalries, and alliances to maintain a balance of power have been tried time and time again and have always failed. Nor have the humanitarian efforts of men of good will been sufficient, without political machinery to implement their ideals. The events of recent years make doubly sure the lesson of history, that there can be no permanent security for free peoples until they organize a Community of Nations wise enough, generous enough, and powerful enough to safeguard and foster their essential liberties. Now, at long last, that lesson is being learned.

Finally, in addition to our advantages in social experience, scientific resources, and economic and political techniques, we have ethical and religious values which were unknown to the Greeks, to enlighten and fortify the spirits of those who believe in democracy. With all this in our favor, there is good reason to believe that the outcome of the struggle to attain and maintain it now can be a far happier one than it was in ancient Athens.

Chronology

(All dates are B.C. unless otherwise specified)

PIONEERS

Trojan War, c. 1200–1180.
Iliad and *Odyssey*, c. 800.
Rise of aristocracies, c. 800–700.
Hesiod, c. 700.
Archilochus, fl. 650.
Alcaeus, fl. 600.
Solon's reforms, 594–593.
Anaximander, fl. 580.
Xenophanes, fl. 540.
Pythagoras, fl. 530.
Theognis, fl. 520.
Heraclitus, fl. 515.
Anacreon, fl. 500.
Rule of Pisistratus, 561–556, 550, 540–528.
Reforms of Cleisthenes, 508–507.

Parmenides, fl. 505.
Simonides, 556–478.
Herodotus, c. 484–425.
Aeschylus, 525–456.
Pindar, c. 522–448.
Battle of Marathon, 490.
Battle of Salamis, 480.

ATHENS: DEMOCRACY AND EMPIRE

Founding of the Delian League, 478.
Removal of the League treasury to Athens, 454.
Pericles' leadership, 461–429.
Peloponnesian War, 431–404.
Pericles' Funeral Speech, 430.
Revolt of Mitylene, 428.
Death of Cleon, 422.
Conquest of Melos, 416.
Sicilian Expedition, 415.
Revolution of the Four Hundred, 411.
Restoration of democracy under Cleophon, 410.
Rule of the Thirty, 404–403.
Thucydides, c. 465–396.
Brygus Painter, fl. 500–480.
Penthesilea Painter, fl. 480–460.
Athenian Treasury at Delphi, c. 500.
Parthenon, 447–432.
Athena Nike Temple, c. 425.
Erechtheum, c. 421.
Myron, fl. 450.

Phidias, fl. 440.

Protagoras forced to leave Athens, 415.

Gorgias, fl. 430.

Socrates, 469–399.

Aeschylus: *Agamemnon, Libation Bearers, Eumenides,* 458.

Sophocles: *Antigone,* 443; *Oedipus the King,* 429; *Electra,* 420–410; *Philoctetes, Oedipus at Colonus,* 410–01.

Euripides: *Alcestis,* 438; *Medea,* 431; *Hippolytus,* 428; *Children of Heracles, Hecuba, Andromache, Suppliant Women,* 430–420; *Mad Heracles, Iphigenia among the Taurians,* 420–410; *Trojan Women,* 415; *Electra,* 413; *Helen,* 412; *Orestes,* 408; *Ion, Bacchae,* 410–01.

THE CRITICISM AND DECLINE OF DEMOCRACY

Aristophanes: *Acharnians,* 425; *Knights,* 424; *Clouds,* 423; *Wasps,* 422; *Peace,* 421; *Birds,* 414; *Lysistrata,* 411; *Thesmophoriazusae,* 410; *Frogs,* 405; *Ecclesiazusae,* 393.

Supremacy of Sparta, 404–371.

Supremacy of Thebes, 371–362.

Philip of Macedon, 383–336.

Alexander the Great, fl. 336–323.

Rome defeats Macedon, 168.

Rome conquers Greece, 146.

Praxiteles, fl. 370–330.

Scopas, fl. 350.

Lysippus, fl. 360–315.

Isocrates, 436–338.

Demosthenes, 384–322.

Plato, 428–347.

Aristotle, 384–322.

Aratus assumes leadership of Achaean League, 251.

Polybius, 210–128.

Diogenes, fl. 330.

Epicurus, fl. 300.

Epictetus, fl. 90 A.D.

NOTES

For the convenience of readers who wish to place in their context the chief passages which have been quoted, the following references are given.

INTRODUCTION

1. *Drift and Mastery* (Mitchell Kennerley), p. 82.
2. *Ethics*, Vol. LI, 1-21.

CHAPTER 1

1. *Iliad*, II, 211-42.
2. *Ibid.*, II, 244-78.
3. *Ibid.*, XVIII, 478-608.

CHAPTER 2

1. *Works and Days*, 207-11.

CHAPTER 3

1. *Timaeus*, 22.
2. Herodotus, I, 30-33.
3. *Ibid.*, VIII, 143.
4. *Ibid.*, V, 78.
5. *Persians*, 402-05.

CHAPTER 4

1. *Thucydides*, II, 6.
2. *Ibid.*
3. *Ibid.*, II, 7.

CHAPTER 5

1. *Athenian Studies Presented to W. S. Ferguson*, p. 470. Quoted by courtesy of the publishers, the Harvard University Press.
2. *Solon and Croesus*, pp. 161-62. Quoted by courtesy of the publishers, the Oxford University Press.

CHAPTER 6

1. Thucydides, III, 9.
2. *Ibid.*
3. *Ibid.*, V, 17.
4. *Ibid.*
5. *Ibid.*
6. *Ibid.*, III, 10.

CHAPTER 7

1. *Pericles*, XIII.

CHAPTER 9

1. *Antigone*, 736-40.

CHAPTER 10

1. *Alcestis*, 962-1005. *The Collected Poems of A. E. Housman* (Henry Holt and Company), pp. 246-47. In a letter to me dated March 22, 1933, Mr. Housman referred to his version as a "Swinburnian translation from Euripides," but it reproduces better than any other the tenderness and dignity of the original. I am indebted to the Estate of A. E. Housman for permission to reprint it here.

CHAPTER 11

1. *Medea*, 225-51.

CHAPTER 12

1. *Odes*, XIII. See also XII.

CHAPTER 13

1. *Acharnians*, 280-85, 305-16, 509-38.
2. *Knights*, 178-94.
3. *Ecclesiazusae*, 217-27.

CHAPTER 14

1. *Philippics*, III.
2. *De Rhod. Lib.*, 17-18.

CHAPTER 15

1. *Laws*, 653-54.
2. *Republic*, 401-2.
3. *Ibid.*, 401.
4. *Ibid.*, 456.

CHAPTER 17

1. *Polybius*, IV, 31.

CHAPTER 18

1. *Discourses*, 4, 1.
2. *Ibid.*, 4, 1; 3, 5.
3. *Ibid.*, 1, 18.
4. *Ibid.*, 3, 24.
5. *Ibid.*, 3, 22.
6. *Ibid.*, 1, 2.

A LIST OF BOOKS FOR

FURTHER READING

This account of Greek democracy inevitably suffers from compression and simplification. In order to build up a three-dimensional picture which will reveal the richer colors of the scene, the subtler gradations of motives and action, and the total complex pattern of events, the reader is urged to continue in the following books.

PREFACE

Among the most important studies of Greek society, Gustav Glotz' *The Greek City and Its Institutions* (Knopf) and Alfred E. Zimmern's *The Greek Commonwealth* (Oxford) trace the development and character of the Greek city-states; Glotz' *Ancient Greece at Work* (Knopf) deals with the economic factors; and Ernest Barker's *Greek Political Theory: Plato and His Predecessors* (Methuen) and *The Political Thought of Plato and Aristotle* (Putnam) analyze the theories of government. Further implications of Greek democracy are discussed in Werner Jaeger's *Paideia* (Blackwell, Oxford), which shows the relation of education in its widest sense to social development; T. B. L. Webster's *Greek Art and Literature* (Oxford), which traces the connection between those two phases of Greek expression; and A. D. Winspear's *The Genesis of Plato's Thought* (Dryden), a suggestive study of the interplay of politics, economics and philosophy.

Standard histories of Greece are the *Cambridge Ancient History* (Cambridge), Vols. IV-VII; J. H. Breasted's *Ancient Times* (Ginn);

J. B. Bury's *A History of Greece* (Macmillan); M. Rostovtzeff's *A History of the Ancient World* (Oxford), Vol. I; and E. M. Sanford's *The Mediterranean World in Ancient Times* (Ronald). For a popular survey see Will Durant's *The Life of Greece* (Simon and Schuster).

CHAPTER 1

Homer: *Iliad*. Translated by A. Lang, W. Leaf and E. Myers (Macmillan); Samuel Butler (Fifield); A. T. Murray (Loeb Classical Library, Harvard University Press); Lord Derby (Everyman's Library, E. P. Dutton and Company).
Homer: *Odyssey*. Translated by S. H. Butcher and A. Lang (Macmillan); T. E. Shaw, "Lawrence of Arabia" (Oxford); Samuel Butler (Fifield); A. T. Murray (Loeb); Cowper (Everyman).

CHAPTER 2

Hesiod: *Works and Days*. Translated by A. W. Mair (Oxford); H. G. Evelyn-White (Loeb).
Lyra Graeca. Translated by J. M. Edmonds (Loeb).
Bakewell, C. M.: *Source-Book in Ancient Philosophy* (Scribner).

CHAPTER 3

Freeman, K.: *The Work and Life of Solon* (Milford).
Plutarch: *Life of Solon*. Translated by B. Perrin (Loeb); Dryden and T. M. Clough (Everyman).
Herodotus: Translated by A. D. Godley (Loeb); George Rawlinson (Everyman).
Aristotle: *Republica Atheniensum*. Translated by F. G. Kenyon (Oxford); H. Rackham (Loeb).

CHAPTERS 4–6

Plutarch: *Life of Pericles*.
Aristotle: *Republica Atheniensum*.
Thucydides: *History of the Peloponnesian War*. Translated by B. Jowett (Oxford); C. F. Smith (Loeb); Richard Crawley (Everyman). A. E. Zimmern's excellent translation of the Funeral Speech is given in his *Greek Commonwealth*, Chapter VIII.
Xenophon: *Hellenica*. Translated by C. L. Brownson (Loeb).

CHAPTER 7

For illustrations to accompany this chapter, see Anderson, W. J., Spiers, R. P., and W. B. Dinsmoor: *The Architecture of Ancient Greece* (Scribner); Richter, G. M. A.: *The Sculpture and Sculptors of the Greeks* (Yale); and Swindler, M. H.: *Ancient Painting* (Yale).

CHAPTER 8

Plato: *Protagoras, Gorgias, Euthydemus.* Translated by B. Jowett (Oxford); W. R. M. Lamb, H. N. Fowler, R. G. Bury and P. Shorey (Loeb).

Plato: *Socratic Discourses of Plato and Xenophon.* Introduction by A. D. Lindsay (Everyman).

CHAPTERS 9 AND 10

Aeschylus: *Tragedies.* Translated by H. W. Smyth (Loeb); J. S. Blackie (Everyman); G. Murray (Oxford). Perhaps the best translation of the *Agamemnon* is the one by Louis MacNeice (Harcourt, Brace).

Sophocles: *Tragedies.* Translated by R. C. Jebb (Cambridge); F. Storr (Loeb); G. Young (Everyman); G. Murray (Oxford).

Euripides: *Tragedies.* Translated by G. Murray (Oxford); A. S. Way (Loeb); Wodhull, Potter, Shelley and Milman (Everyman).

CHAPTER 11

Euripides: *Medea, Trojan Women, Hecuba, Andromache.*

Aristophanes: *Thesmophoriazusae.* Translated by B. B. Rogers (Loeb); J. H. Frere (Everyman).

Murray, G.: *Five Stages of Greek Religion* (Oxford).

Nilsson, M. P.: *A History of Greek Religion* (Oxford).

CHAPTER 12

Bacchylides: *Lyra Graeca.*

Sophocles: *Oedipus at Colonus.*

Euripides: *Hippolytus, Mad Heracles, Suppliant Women.*

For illustrations see the books listed under Chapter 7.

CHAPTER 13

Xenophon: *Oeconomicus*. Translated by E. C. Marchant (Loeb).
Pindar: *Odes*. Translated by J. E. Sandys (Loeb).
Aristophanes: *Comedies*. Translated by B. B. Rogers, J. H. Frere.
Bakewell, C. M.: *Source-Book in Ancient Philosophy*.

CHAPTER 14

Aeschines. Translated by C. D. Adams (Loeb).
Demosthenes. Translated by A. W. Pickard-Cambridge (Oxford); J. H.
     and C. A. Vince (Loeb).
Plutarch: *Life of Demosthenes*.
Isocrates. Translated by G. B. Norlin (Loeb).

CHAPTER 15

Plato: *Republic, Statesman, Laws*. Translated by B. Jowett (Oxford);
     A. D. Lindsay (Everyman); P. Shorey (Loeb).

CHAPTER 16

Aristotle: *Politics*. Translated by B. Jowett (Oxford); H. Rackham
     (Loeb); W. Ellis (Everyman).

CHAPTER 17

Polybius: *History*. Translated by W. R. Paton (Loeb).

CHAPTER 18

Livingstone, R. L.: *The Mission of Greece* (Oxford).
Epicurus. Translated by C. Bailey (Oxford).
Epictetus: *Discourses*. Translated by P. E. Matheson (Oxford); W. A.
     Oldfather (Loeb); E. Carter (Everyman).

Index

Achaean League, 101, 235-238, 262
Achaeans, Homeric, 20
Acharnians, 183-186, 261, 265
Achilles, 20, 21, 24, 26, 28, 33
Admetus, 144, 145
Administration, public, in Athens, 51, 60, 70, 71, 74, 75
Aeschines, 199, 200, 202, 203, 270
Aeschylus, 54, 127, 128, 129, 130, 131, 132, 134, 137, 143, 146, 148, 167, 260, 261, 269
Aetolian League, 234, 235, 236
Agamemnon, 19-22, 28, 147, 150
Agamemnon, 137, 146, 261, 269
Aidos, moral principle of, 27, 28, 31
Ajax, 137, 148, 150
Alcaeus, 37, 38, 259
Alcestis, 144, 145, 150, 261, 264
Alcibiades, 93
Alexander the Great, 203, 205, 232, 233, 235, 261
Aliens, resident, 69, 76, 79, 81, 103, 154, 219, 227, 256
Amazons, 111, 163, 165, 167, 169
Amphictyonic League, 230, 231
Anacreon, 39, 259
Anaxagoras, 42, 64, 66, 160
Anaximander, 41, 259
Andromache, 27

Andromache, 131, 138, 155, 261, 269
Antigone, 132, 133, 149
Antigone, 130, 132, 143, 261, 264
Antisthenes, 241, 243
Aphrodite, 110, 141, 146, 149
Apollo, 141, 144, 146, 149, 150, 164, 211, 218, 230
Aratus, 236, 238, 262
Arcadian League, 233, 234
Archilochus, 37, 259
Architecture, fifth-century Athenian, 107-113; Doric, 108; Ionic, 108; fourth-century Athenian, 196
Archons, 71
Areopagus, 132, 161
Aristides, 84, 132
Aristocrats, attitude of, toward democracy, 3, 4, 176, 179-193; tribal, 27, 28; during transitional period, 31, 34-39, 44, 49, 50; in fifth-century Athens, 59, 66, 81, 82, 93-95, 99, 121; in fourth-century Athens, 98, 206; Plato on, 217; Aristotle on, 222, 223
Aristophanes, 86, 128, 157, 182-192, 196, 261, 270
Aristotle, 137, 141, 142, 155, 221-228, 245, 262, 268, 270

Art, Homeric, 24; sixth-century Athenian, 50; fifth-century Athenian, 61, 82, 102-115; fourth-century Athenian, 196; social function of, 211, 212-214, 224. *See also* Architecture; Sculpture; Vases

Asia Minor, 23, 30, 83, 194, 235

Aspasia, 64, 66, 185

Assembly, Homeric, 25, 26; Athenian, 51, 59, 67, 70, 71, 72, 73, 75, 87, 90, 118, 180; Spartan, 177; in confederacies, 233, 234

Athena, 108, 109, 110, 111, 112, 113, 132, 146, 166, 171

Athenian Treasury, Delphi, 108, 111, 166, 260

Athens, unification of, 45; progress under Solon, 45, 46; progress under Pisistratus, 49, 50; progress under Cleisthenes, 50, 51; defeats Persia, 51, 52, 54-56; Pericles' ideals for, 59-68; fifth-century democracy of, 69-82; governs an empire, 83-101, 231; in the Peloponnesian War, 87-97; art in, 102-115; education in, 116-126; glorified in tragedies, 129-131; intolerance in, 152-161; devotion to Theseus, 162-171; conservatives in 175-193; in the fourth century, 195-205

Atomic theory, 42

Attica, 45, 67, 198

Autocracy, attitude toward democracy, 3, 4; methods of, 5, 13; industrial, 8, 13; of Philip of Macedon, 202, 205

Bacchae, 150, 161, 261

Bacchylides, 165, 166, 269

Barbarians, 139, 154, 200, 219

Birds, 189, 261

Boeotia, 31, 231

Brandeis, Louis, 10

Brygus, 105, 260

Business interests, tribal, 25; seventh-century, 35, 36; sixth-century, 36, 49-51; fifth-century, 70, 76, 78, 80, 95, 104, 154, 159, 187; fourth-century, 195, 199; Plato's conception of, 210, 214, 215; Aristotle's conception of, 228

Callicrates, 103

Cannon, Dr. Walter B., 12

Censorship, 10, 182, 212, 214

Centaurs, 111, 163, 165

Chaeronea, 204

Chalcidice, league of, 233

Change, theories of, 40-43, 213, 214

Children of Heracles, 136, 261

Chorus, in tragedies, 131, 141, 144, 146

Cimon, 73, 131, 167

Citizenship in Athens, 69-75

Civil liberties, as dynamic functions, 9. *See also* Freedom

Class war, 35-39, 49, 93-97, 195

Cleisthenes, 50, 51, 259

Cleon, 88, 89, 171, 186, 187, 188, 191, 204, 260

Cleophon, 97, 260

Cleophrades painter, 106

Clouds, 189, 190, 191, 261

Clytemnestra, 137, 147

Comedy, 182-192, 196

Commercial class, in tribal society, 25; in the seventh century, 35; in the sixth century, 49; in the fifth century, 86; in the fourth century, 195, 225. *See also* Business interests

Communications, system of, 100, 256, 257

Communism, 177, 215

Confederations. *See* Achaean League; Aetolian League; Amphictyonic League; Boeotia; Chalcidice; Corinth; Delian League; Peloponnesian League

Co-operation, cultural value of, 4, 12, 113, 257

Corinth, 86, 87, 100, 129, 232

Council, tribal, 25; Athenian, 51, 70, 71, 73, 74, 96; federal, 83, 233, 234, 235; Spartan, 177

Courage, tribal, 26; of Solon, 49; Pericles' conception of, 61, 62; Plato's conception of, 214; Stoic, 250

Courts, law, 46, 70, 71, 73, 83-86, 118, 124, 235

Craftsmen, 24, 25, 35, 50, 51, 65, 70, 76, 80, 103, 104, 154, 177, 213

Creon, 132, 133, 143, 149

Cresilas, 114

Crete, 29

Critias, 124

Croesus, 48, 264

Custom, influence of, 54, 73, 179, 180, 192, 243

Cynics, 241-244

Damonides, 64, 66

Debts, cancelled by Solon, 45; in fifth-century Athens, 73

Delian League, 83, 84, 197, 231, 260

Delphi, 56, 108, 167, 230, 231

Demagogues, 137, 192, 224, 225

Demeter, 34

Democracy, definition of, 3, 14; criticism of, by autocrats and aristocrats, 3, 4; principles of, 5-16, 119; tribal, 23-26; progress under Solon, 45, 46; progress under Pisistratus, 49-50; progress under Cleisthenes, 50, 51; defense of, in Herodotus, 52-53; Pericles' conception of, 60-63; in fifth-century Athens, 69-82, 182; in the Athenian empire, 90, 91, 100, 101; influence on art, 102, 103; criticized by Socrates, 124, 125; appraised by the tragedians, 175-193; criticized by Athenian aristocrats, 175-193; in the fourth century, 97, 196; Plato's appraisal of, 206, 216; Aristotle's appraisal of, 222-225; in confederations, 231-237; Stoic, 244; contemporary, 256-258

Democritus, 42

Demos, 186, 187

Demosthenes, General, 186, 187

Demosthenes, orator, 81, 197-204, 262, 270

Destiny, 26, 140-151, 246

Dicaeopolis, 183, 184, 185

Diodotus, 88, 90

Diogenes, 242-244, 262

Dionysus, 33, 128, 135, 150

Divorce, 81, 158

Dorians, 45, 176

Doric architecture, 108

Ecclesiazusae, 190, 191, 261, 265

Education, democratic, 7, 15, 257; Athenian, 60, 104, 116-126, 186, 189, 190; Spartan, 178; Plato's theory of, 211-215, 219; Aristotle's theory of, 227; Stoic, 245

Egypt, 46, 113, 155, 214, 235, 236

Eleatic philosophers, 42-44

Electra, 134, 150, 261

Eleusinian Mysteries, 34

Empedocles, 42

Empire, Athenian, 83-101

Enterprise, private, 11, 48, 61, 76; public, 15, 61, 71, 72

Ephors, 177

Epictetus, 245-251, 262, 270
Epicurus, 240, 241, 262, 270
Equality, democratic theory of, 11; in sixth-century Athens, 51; in fifth-century Athens, 52, 60, 180; Plato's theory of, 208; Aristotle's theory of, 223
Erechtheum, 112, 113, 260
Eubulus, 199
Eumenides, 132, 146, 261
Euripides, 127, 128, 129, 130, 134, 137, 138, 139, 143, 146, 147, 149, 155, 158, 161, 167, 171, 190, 261, 269
Exile, 153
Experts, use of, by democracies, 4, 9, 12, 13; demanded by Plato, 207

Family, 48, 132
Farmers, status of, tribal, 24; in the seventh century, 25, 31-32; in fifth-century Athens, 66, 67, 70, 176
Fate, 140-151
Festivals, 50, 60, 65, 72, 77, 82, 167, 180, 198
Freedom, of speech, 5, 9, 10, 14, 62, 63, 81, 131, 153, 208, 237; artistic, 5, 109; religious, 5, 14, 161; economic, 5, 14, 76, 79; in fifth-century Athens, 52, 61, 62, 67, 71, 78, 81, 140-151, 152; in the Athenian Empire, 84, 85, 87; Demosthenes on, 202; Plato on, 208, 209, 218; Aristotle on, 223, 224; Epicurean conception of, 241; Cynic conception of, 242; Stoic conception of, 246, 249, 250
Frieze, sculptural, 111, 112
Frogs, 128, 190, 261

Generals, 51, 59, 71, 72, 93, 208, 234, 236

Gods, 26, 32, 33, 42, 92, 104, 112, 114, 119, 141, 142, 147, 148, 149, 159, 168, 190, 218, 240, 247, 248, 249, 250
Gorgias, 120, 261, 269
Gymnasia, 117, 138, 164

Haemon, 133, 134
Hector, 27
Hecuba, 136, 146, 149
Helots, 176, 177
Helen of Troy, 156, 163, 164
Heracles, 108, 130, 141, 145, 163, 165, 166, 168, 169, 170
Heraclitus, 41, 259
Herodotus, 48, 52, 53, 155, 260, 263, 268
Hesiod, 31, 32, 41, 156, 163, 164, 259, 268
Hippias, 120
Hippocrates, 42
Hippodamus, 107
Hippolytus, 136, 141, 161, 169, 170, 171, 261, 269
Holmes, Oliver Wendell, 10
Homer, 19, 32, 41, 268
Hospitality, 27, 147
Housman, A. E., 144, 264
Hybris (pride), 52, 54, 143, 154

Ibycus, 39
Ictinus, 103
Idealism in art, 115
Iliad, 19, 23, 25, 26, 28, 50, 143, 156, 163, 259, 263, 268
Immortality, 33, 34
Impressionism in art, 115
International relations, democratic, 16, 257; Athenian, 83-101; in the fourth century, 194-205, 232-238; Plato's theory of, 219; Aristotle's theory of, 227, 228; in confederations, 229-238
Intolerance, racial, 7, 154, 155; religious, 7, 159-161; national, 154; sexual, 156-159

Ion, 136, 161
Ionia, 40, 164
Ionic architecture, 108
Iphigenia among the Taurians, 148, 261
Iphigenia at Aulis, 138, 150
Isocrates, 199, 200, 232, 262, 270
Italiot Greece, 29, 42, 43

Jason, 149, 155, 158, 159
Jefferson, Thomas, 13
Jocasta, 148
Juries, Athenian, 51, 71, 73, 189
Justice, theories of, by Hesiod, 32; by Solon, 47; in fifth-century Athens, 74, 121; in the Athenian empire, 90; by Plato, 209, 210; by Aristotle, 227; by Epicurus, 241; Stoic, 250

Kings, 22, 24-26, 52, 177, 238, 249
Knights, 186, 187, 261, 265
Knowledge, Socrates' theory of, 123, 124

Lamachus, 185
Lapiths, 111, 163
Law, Solon's conception of, 47; Athenian, 60, 73; in the Athenian empire, 85, 86, 88; international, 219
Laws, 208, 212, 217, 265, 270
Leadership, democratic, 13; of Solon, 46-49; of Pisistratus, 49; of Cleisthenes, 50; of Pericles, 64-68; of Cleon, 88-90; of Demosthenes, 204
Leuctra, 237
Libation Bearers, 147, 261
Liberty, 5, 6, 52, 68, 79, 131, 208, 218, 223. See also Freedom
Lincoln, Abraham, 136
Lippmann, Walter, 8
Lot, in elections, 51, 70, 71, 72, 74, 181, 199, 207, 218

Lydia, 48
Lyric poetry, 37-39
Lysippus, 196, 261
Lysistrata, 188, 189, 261

Macedon, 97, 194, 197, 200, 201, 229, 230, 232, 235, 236, 238, 239, 261
Majority, decisions by the, 10, 11, 72
Marathon, 51, 54, 129, 167, 260
Marriage, 81, 190, 218, 243
Mathematics, 43, 117, 179, 214
Medea, 129, 155, 261, 264, 269
Megara, 38, 39, 185
Meidias, 106
Meiklejohn, Donald, 10
Melos, 91, 92, 121, 138, 260
Mercantile class, tribal, 25; in the seventh century, 35; in the sixth century, 37, 44, 49; in fifth-century Athens, 68, 96; in fourth-century Athens, 195
Metics, 69, 76, 79, 81, 103, 153, 218
Metopes, 111
Micon, 167
Middle class, 137, 191, 225, 226
Miltiades, 73
Mimnermus, 37
Mine workers, 78
Minorities, treatment of, by majorities, 9; in Athens, 72, 152, 153; Aristotle on, 225, 226
Mitylene, 37, 38, 87-90, 233, 260
Monarchy, 53, 217, 222
Money, 35, 46, 48
Murray, Gilbert, 127, 269
Music, 72, 117, 211, 212
Myron, 103, 114, 260
Mysteries, religious, 33, 34, 40, 160

Nausicaä, 24
Navy, 52, 96, 197, 231
Nebraska State Capitol, 113

Neoptolemus, 134, 150
Nicias, 73

Odysseus, 20-22, 24, 27, 134
Odyssey, 23-25, 27, 28, 33, 50, 156, 163, 259, 268
Oedipus, 129, 141, 168, 169, 171
Oedipus at Colonus, 130, 261, 269
Oedipus the King, 134, 146, 148, 261
Old Oligarch, 180, 181
Oligarchy, defense of, 53; in fifth-century Athens, 96, 97; Spartan, 176-179; Plato on, 216, 218; Aristotle on, 223
Olympia, 167, 230, 243
Olynthus, 233
Oracles, 56, 147
Orestes, 136, 141, 147, 148
Orphic religion, 34, 41, 43
Ostracism, 153

Painting, 104-106, 196, 214
Panathenaea, 50, 111, 164
Pandora, 156
Parmenides, 43, 260
Parthenon, 108-112, 167, 260
Pausanias, 164
Pay for public service, 65, 72, 96
Peace, 188, 261
Peace, 67, 98, 137, 139, 198, 249
Pediments, 110, 111
Peloponnesian League, 231; War, 87-97
Pentheus, 148, 150
Pericles, 42, 59-69, 76, 80, 87, 95, 100, 102, 114, 116, 129, 133, 134, 136, 151, 153, 157, 160, 169, 171, 185, 188, 204, 228, 255, 260, 264, 268
Perioeci, 176, 177
Persephone, 34
Persia, 52, 54, 55, 83, 84, 96, 97, 131, 155, 160, 181, 194, 199, 200, 204, 208, 231, 232, 233
Persians, 54, 128, 263

Phidias, 64, 66, 103, 109, 110, 167, 261
Philip of Macedon, 195, 197-205, 231, 232, 261
Philoctetes, 134, 150, 261
Philosophy, in Ionia, 40-42; in Italiot Greece, 42, 43; Sophists, 117-121; Socrates, 122-125; Plato, 206-220; Aristotle, 221-228; Epicureans, 240, 241; Cynics, 241-244; Stoics, 244-250
Phoenician Maidens, 150
Pindar, 179, 260, 270
Pisistratus, 47, 49, 50, 53, 104, 105, 163, 164, 171, 259
Pittacus, 38
Plague, at Athens, 67, 68, 98, 99
Plataea, 54, 55
Plato, 46, 206-220, 221, 226, 227, 262, 269, 270
Plutarch, 46, 64, 65, 107, 132, 170, 268, 270
Poetics, 141, 142
Police, 79
Politicians, 134, 195
Politics, 222, 270
Polybius, 236, 237, 238, 262, 265, 270
Polycrates, 39
Polygnotus, 106
Polytheism, 161
Population, of Athens, 69, 70; of Sparta, 177
Poseidon, 110, 166, 167, 168, 184
Praxiteles, 196, 261
Priests, 34, 46, 147, 161
Priscus Helvidius, 250, 251
Prodicus, 120
Prometheus, 148
Property, private, 24, 48, 215
Protagoras, 119, 122, 160, 261, 269
Public works projects, 50, 65, 77, 85, 97, 107, 180, 196

Punishment, Plato's theory of, 219
Pythagoreans, 42, 43, 179, 180
Pythian games, 230

Realism in art, 106, 115, 196
Refugees, 129
Religion, Homeric, 25; in the seventh century, 33, 34; Dionysiac mysteries, 33, 34; Orphic mysteries, 34, 41, 43; attacked by philosophers, 41; attitude of dramatists toward, 141-143, 146-151; intolerance in, 159-161; importance of, 159, 160; attitude of Epicureans toward, 240, 241; attitude of Cynics toward, 243; attitude of Stoics toward, 247, 248
Representative government, 8, 70
Republic, 209-217, 265, 270
Restraints on liberty, 6, 73
Revolution, 36, 45, 47, 93-95, 222, 223, 228, 260
Rights, personal, 5, 6, 120, 121
Rome, 205, 229, 235, 236, 237, 238, 239, 245, 261

Salamis, 51, 54, 128, 131, 260
Sappho, 37
Science, 117, 122, 256
Scopas, 196, 261
Sculpture, 103, 113-115, 196, 214
Security, economic, 77
Semonides, 157
Seven against Thebes, 132
Sexual intolerance, 156-159
Sicilian expedition, 92, 93, 138, 188, 260
Simonides, 54, 55, 260
Skepticism, 118, 176
Slavery, tribal, 24, 27; sixth-century, 35; Athenian, 70, 73, 76-82, 101, 103, 120, 153, 155, 180; Euripides on, 135; Spartan, 177; Plato on, 218; Aristotle on, 227, 228; Epictetus on, 246
Social contract theory, 209, 241
Socrates, 122-125, 153, 154, 161, 181, 189, 190, 191, 206, 207, 261
Solon, 45-49, 171, 199, 204, 225, 259, 264, 268
Sophists, 117-122, 124, 160, 161, 207, 209, 240
Sophocles, 127, 129, 130, 132, 133, 134, 137, 143, 146, 149, 167, 261, 269
Sparta, 66, 67, 87, 91, 92, 93, 96, 97, 99, 100, 130, 153, 176-179, 183, 184, 188, 189, 192, 194, 195, 197, 200, 217, 229, 231, 236, 243, 261
Statesman, 217, 270
Stoics, 244-251
Suppliants, 131, 146
Suppliant Women, 130, 135, 136, 138, 168, 169, 261, 269

Taxation, 77, 198, 199, 208, 225
Temples, 107, 108, 112, 113, 164
Thebes, 87, 129, 130, 194, 195, 197, 204, 205, 229, 232, 233, 261
Themistocles, 52
Theognis, 38, 259
Theramenes, 96, 97
Thermopylae, 54
Thersites, 20-23, 26
Theseus, 45, 108, 130, 135, 149, 162-171
Thesmophoriazusae, 157, 190, 261, 269
Thucydides, 60, 64, 66, 68, 84, 88, 93, 168, 260, 264, 268
Timaeus, 46, 263
Tiresias, 148, 150
Tragedy, 127-151, 196
Tribal society, 23-29

Trojan Women, 138, 146, 155, 261, 269

Troy, 19, 20, 21, 155

Tyranny, compared to a tumor, 12; Solon's judgment of, 47; in the Athenian empire, 100; of Macedon, 197, 202; Plato's appraisal of, 216, 217; Aristotle's appraisal of, 222; Epictetus on, 249

Tyrants, sixth-century, 36-39, 49, 50, 52; the Thirty, 97, 125, 260

Tyrtaeus, 178

Unity, democratic, 13, 14; Greek, 188, 200, 203, 204

Utilities, public, 72

Vases, Athenian, 104-106

Vespasian, 250, 251

War, Trojan, 19-24, 259; Persian, 51-56; Peloponnesian, 87-97, 99, 100, 183, 260; Thucydides on effects of, 93, 94; dramatists' attitude toward, 137, 138, 139, 183-186; Macedonian, 197-205; democracy and, 257

Wasps, 189, 261

Westermann, W. L., 80

Whitman, Walt, 23

Women, status of, in tribal society, 156; in the seventh century, 156; in fifth-century Athens, 63, 81, 82, 120, 157-159; in tragedy, 158, 159; in comedy, 157, 158, 188, 189, 190, 191; according to Plato, 215; according to Aristotle, 228

Xenophanes, 41

Xenophon, 81, 181, 268, 269, 270

Xerxes, 54, 147

Zeno, Eleatic, 43; Stoic, 244

Zeus, 26, 32, 33, 55, 110, 114, 141, 146, 149, 167, 246

Zeuxis, 106

Zimmern, A. E., 80, 267, 268